Give Sorrow Words

Lynn Keane
Give Sorrow Words

*"Give sorrow words; the grief that
does not speak, Whispers the o'er-fraught
heart and bids it break."*
William Shakespeare, *Macbeth, 4.3*

Foreword

Several years ago, some friends lost their daughter to suicide. Soon after, Lynn Keane approached me and asked if I would help her write her story about her twenty-three-year-old son, Daniel, who took his own life. I immediately said yes. And I want everyone to feel the same urgent compulsion about Lynn Keane's timely, beautiful and hope-giving memoir.

Contemporary life is bubbling over with stories about young people taking their lives. Nobody seems to know why. For a parent, losing a child is the most devastating psychic blow they could receive. For a society, losing a child means the loss of a potential citizen whose creativity may have improved the way we live. In Lynn's case, there were no obvious warning signs that her son was in trouble.

To the outside world, Daniel seemed to be a charming and optimistic young man. He and his mother had a loving relationship that most parents would envy. And yet one terrible April night, Daniel had lost hope.

The shock and the loss overwhelmed Lynn and her family. In *Give Sorrow Words* she tells us about the clues she and her husband didn't understand while their son was alive. And step-by-step, she shows us how her family reconstructed their lives without Daniel. This isn't a tabloid tale about neglectful parents abusing their child. Lynn and her family were like many North American families who are committed to loving one another despite predictable family tensions and struggles. For that reason alone, her touching and lyrical memoir is an important social document of our times. Lynn is us. Read what she has to say. We need to hear it.

Susan Swan 2012

to my family

This edition published in 2014 by Starburst DRI

c/o Transatlantic Literary Agency Inc.

2 Bloor Street East, Suite 3500

Toronto, Ontario

M4W 1A8

ISBN 978-0-9880703-7-0

Cover Image & Book Design by Angel Guerra@angeljohnguerra.com

Printed in the United States of America

Library and Archives Canada Cataloguing in Publication

Keane, Lynn, 1958-, author

Give sorrow words / Lynn Keane.

Issued in print and electronic formats.

ISBN 978-0-9880703-7-0 (pbk.).--ISBN 978-0-9880703-6-3 (html)

1. Depression, Mental. 2. Depressed persons--Family relationships.

3. Suicide victims--Family relationships. . Children--Death. I. Title.

RC537.K43 2014   616.85'270092   C2013-908411-8

C2013-908412-6

Contents

Prelude

Letter to Daniel (part one)

My Dearest Daniel,

In the days since you've been away from me I have had time to reflect and remember what a joy it was to be with you. You have left me with pieces of yourself, parts of you, that I hold close. You and I were inseparable for most of your life. Your signature was always your warm, infectious smile. A daydreamer, you were. Always thinking as you gazed out a window. What was out there that I could not see?

We talked often about lyrics and their significance in the greater scheme. You were intuitive and understood the depth of emotion that was knotted within the subtext of a song.

I lie awake most mornings and remember you; your last birthday, when you turned twenty-three and you sent an email, reminding me what you wanted to eat for your birthday dinner. I even think of your Rice Dream milk that was in the refrigerator the week you vanished. My brain stacks the memories and yearnings together. You were full of energy and you were moving toward a bright future.

You have also left me with an understanding of human misery. In death, you have shown me how the human spirit works to transform itself, although not always successfully. My mind works overtime reaching out to you. Daniel, your family misses you. Some days we feel as if we are sinking in sand, the ground beneath us falling away. We are full of sorrow.

I laughed in your company and was never happier than when we were all together as a family of five. I remember being in the kitchen as you prepared an epic meal for us, talking and making plans for our next great family adventure. I was extremely proud of the man you had become. As mothers and sons go, we selected well...

Attachment

Our family is drawn to water; perhaps it fulfills a longing to be on the edge of something vast and filled with mystery.

Chapter 1

The Last Photograph

Bonita Beach, Florida, March 12, 2010
I'm sitting on the creamy white sand of Bonita Beach, where Daniel and my family played beach Frisbee just a year ago. Once you make your way past the low-lying matted grasses and brush swaying in the breeze, the majesty of the Gulf of Mexico extends as far as the eye can see. Sandcastles dot the strip of coast stretching from Naples in the south to Fort Myers at the northern tip.

The landscape of southwestern Florida reminds me of Nantucket or Maine, but as I breathe in the sunshine and salt air it strikes me that nothing I'm seeing will last. Nature will morph into something else. The sandpipers and pelicans flying in and out of the surf will vanish, and the shore with its scattering of ragged seashells will erode with the tides. Each of us is alive but a moment. There is impermanence to everything. We are here and then we are gone.

I can't help staring at the families relaxing on the shore. Children's voices pierce the thick sea air. Grandparents shepherd their grandchildren up and down the beach while greedy seagulls fight over the food wrappers left by beachgoers. One tall lean boy stands out. His frame is strong and his hair is dark and curly. His honey-brown skin reminds me of Daniel. Daniel had that same olive skin, which turns a rich golden brown in the sun. As I watch, the boy wades into the sea carrying a small surfboard. He tosses the board down and it smacks the surface of the water. At the right moment, he heaves himself onto the board to catch a short ride above the waves. He is dedicated to his pursuit; perhaps it gives him a boost of adrenalin. He continues surfing for a long time up and down the beach, and I raise my small black notebook to block out my view of the boy. He looks too much like my son. Daniel also liked the rush of moving quickly over the surface of the water. He required adrenalin too.

. . . .

Bonita Beach, Florida, March 14, 2009
On Emily's fifteenth birthday, in March of 2009, our family made plans to spend the afternoon on the ocean not far from where I'm sitting now. The coolers were loaded and the beach toys and towels were stuffed into the stowage lockers of our boat. We had decided to head out for an afternoon on the warm waters of the Gulf of Mexico, followed by a picnic on the beach. Excited, we drove our truck to the marina, not knowing that the memory of our picnic would soon become bittersweet.

After hours of floating on the indigo sea, soaking up the sun, Bruce turned off the engine and we dropped anchor near the beach. We gently rocked back and forth in the waves while Daniel walked up to the bow of the boat and flipped open the hatch where the anchor was stored. He hauled up the heavy iron anchor and tossed it into the sea.

My son packed most of our gear on top of his head, stepped off of the transom of the boat and waded to shore. I will never forget his look of exasperation when he realized his family was still on board.

"C'mon, Mom, you're supposed to be a triathlete and you can't even swim twenty feet to shore?" Daniel shouted. "Aimee and Em, jump in! I can't believe I have to carry all of this stuff myself."

Over the years, our family had come to depend on Daniel. Our son was a complex blend of talent and impatience, a natural troubleshooter whose "let's do it" rationale let him jump in and fix an appliance that had stopped working, or label the contents of every plastic container in our garage so we would know where to find all of our family's paraphernalia. On top of one of the bins stacked in our garage there's still the map that Daniel drew to show where we should place our Christmas lights in our yard. Sometimes when I am in the garage I look up and see the handwritten labels that he carefully taped to each bin, and think about how he continues to look out for his family. So it would be wrong to suggest that we took Daniel for granted; we were just very comfortable with him taking the lead.

After Daniel's teasing, we gathered up what was left on the boat and jumped into the refreshing sea, making our way towards our "Captain DK." That March day, I felt as if I knew real happiness. We played beach Frisbee, and when it became too hot to stand a moment longer on the burning sand, we dashed into the foamy waves. I rushed after my two teenage daughters and my son, thrilled by their willingness to spend holiday time with their parents. We seemed to make each other better just by being in one another's company. There seemed to be no end to our togetherness as far as my family was concerned.

When we came out of the ocean, an older couple strolled by in the fading daylight and offered to photograph us. The man complimented our family, adding that we had produced a "unique blend of attractive children." Perhaps from his point of view we represented a model family, blessed with unconditional love.

I also took several photographs of our kids on that March day. In my first photographs, their toes are buried beneath a thin layer of white sand on the shell-encrusted beach. The sky at dusk casts a shimmery ribbon of purple and orange above the calm sea while the tide moves gently away from shore. In the foreground, my three young adult children stare out into the vastness of the Gulf, as if they saw their future on the horizon. Each figure is almost perfectly equidistant from the other and all three are on their feet; the oldest girl stands crossed-legged while the younger one waves a hand in the air. The young man with the upright posture is pointing his fingers toward the sand in an inverted peace sign. A moment caught on my digital camera. The flip side of this image was taken minutes after the luminous sun had faded into the sea.

In the second photo, my kids are sitting on the warm sand, looking at me, their photographer. The young woman with the shining eyes gives me a generous smile. She has spent a day on the beach with her family and she can't hide her joy. She is sensitive and kind, wiser than her years. The teenage girl on the other side of Daniel has pink painted nails, and her hair is a mass of windswept curls. The baby of our family, she is our family peacemaker because she sees both sides of every story. She loves animals. Next to her Daniel sits on top of a colourful surfboard. A Bud Light beer rests nearby on the sand. His sandals are covered in a putty mix of sand and water, his sunburnt toes barely visible. He wears brown board shorts, and his legs are covered with insect bites and bruises. His head is tilted as he looks into the lens of the camera, his smile taut. His creased brow and staring eyes catch me, making me think he loathed the whole process. However, at sunset that day he went along with what his mom wanted him to do. The sense of togetherness that day was too powerful for him to refuse. Our three grown children had each other's backs. As parents we had raised our children to become strong allies and have compassion for others.

These photographs were never meant to be critically analyzed. It was a moment in our family history—an image that will stand through the years as a testament to the raw beauty of family experience. We don't see the darkened corners of our lives through these images. The bits of life and the pieces that pull us along and apart aren't visible to the eye in this photograph.

Daniel, Fort Myers, Florida, March 15, 2009
When Aimee and I got to Florida on Thursday night, I was feeling good, glad to see everyone. Had a lot of fun hanging out that weekend. On Sunday morning I woke up

feeling empty. The same old feelings I'd been having for a while. I didn't want to talk to anyone. When I walked into the kitchen, everyone was eating breakfast and talking. It sounded like birds chattering. I said hi, drank some juice, and left the kitchen. My thoughts were all over the place.

, , , ,

At the beach, I begin writing, and for a while I almost forget the young surfer who resembles my son. Glancing up from my notes I catch his striking profile. He's kneeling on the sand very close to my chair, taking a picture for a group of vacationers. He's just like my son, friendly and accommodating. That's enough. I can't continue watching him.

Chapter Two

Motherhood and Magical Thinking

Milton, December 1987

In early December, thick sticky snowflakes flung themselves at the windows of our home in the rural hamlet of Milton Heights. Daniel was twenty-one months old and we were looking forward to Christmas. On that blustery Saturday morning I dressed Daniel in his blue and white snowsuit with little bunny ears that peeked out from the top of the hood.

"Daniel, Daddy and Mommy are going to take you to find a Christmas tree today. Would you like to help us?"

He responded with a big smile, and then he wiggled off my knee and headed towards the side door yelling, "Dada, Momma, go!"

At the tree farm, I followed Bruce up and down the hills carrying Daniel in my arms, searching for our tree. When we found the perfect tree the farm staff helped us drag it to our car, and then tied it to the roof. The next day Bruce hauled the tree out of the garage where it had been drying out overnight, and set it up in the corner of the family room in front of the glass patio doors. While we put the ornaments on the tree Daniel sat on the floor playing with his toys, pointing to the twinkling lights on the tall evergreen.

The sight of the bright lights that had magically appeared on the tree captivated him.

Soon Daniel began coughing. High-pitched wheezing sounds came from his mouth as he struggled to breathe. We had no idea that he was allergic to trees. Daniel started to cry as his tiny chest heaved up and down.

Bruce and I took Daniel to the Milton Hospital where the emergency room doctor told us that our son was having an asthma attack. The doctor quickly placed a mask over Daniel's nose and mouth. Bruce and I stood there in the emergency room, holding onto our son and waiting for instructions. Watching our son's laboured breathing was frightening, and we had no idea then that Daniel was also developing life-threatening allergies (anaphylaxis) to nuts, dairy, and eggs.

When they released Daniel later that day, we purchased a portable ventilator so we could give him his medication at home. The grey ventilator, with its clear plastic cylinder and green spindly tubing turned out to be Daniel's saviour. But the mask and the machine's throbbing noises scared him. He would run away when I told him it was time for his medication. "Mommy, no."

"Daniel, I want you to take in big breaths like this." I demonstrated what I wanted him to do by swallowing several deep breaths myself. Although I had no idea what it felt like to gasp for air, I knew that the more deeply he breathed in the Ventolin the sooner he would feel better. I learned to become Daniel's advocate and perhaps that's why we were so uniquely tethered to one another, a bond that would last all his life.

Months later, I noticed that Daniel had developed dark circles under his eyes; a telltale sign of someone who has allergies.

"Daniel, don't rub your eyes, honey."

"They're itchy."

"Mommy is going to get your eye drops, okay? I'll be right back, so don't rub your eyes."

I used drops to relieve Daniel's allergic reactions to household dust and pollen. It seemed that he was sensitive to most irritants in the environment. As a result I was stressed out from worrying that I wasn't doing enough. When he had an asthma attack I took it personally; I shouldn't have let him play with that child who had a cold. I berated myself and became obsessed with keeping him healthy. I stopped seeing friends. Daniel and I became comrades in a war against his chronic, life-threatening conditions.

His asthma medication made him jittery, which made it hard for Daniel to concentrate on one task at time. My job was to bring order during these stressful times. In the mornings we would take long walks around Mill Pond, stopping frequently to count the fish in the pond or find rocks to add to his collection at home.

At the time I had a small graphic design business that I ran from home and when Daniel slept during the afternoon I worked on my clients' projects. When his asthma flared up, our routine collapsed. I dived into protective mode, ensuring that he had his medicine at the proper intervals, rest, and fresh air. Sometimes in the afternoon when Daniel was not feeling well, I'd put him down for a nap and find a blanket to cover myself while I lay on the floor beside his bed. His super-mom would save him. One time I remember falling into a deep sleep and then waking up to see Daniel staring down at me on the floor.

"Momma, Ernie."

He wanted his book about Ernie from Sesame Street. I picked Daniel up from his bed and set him on the floor near the window with his book. I wanted him to see the mid-afternoon CN train when it came through. "The train," he'd say.

"I see it too, Daniel."

While Daniel and I sat in his room, the rest of the world seemed far away. All that mattered was my little boy, and what was happening in the pages of his favourite storybook. I held Daniel close to me as his chest heaved up and down; the noise of his exhales and inhales sounding like a broken whistle.

As time went on I became more comfortable with getting in the faces of doctors and nurses who weren't helpful. My purpose was clear: Keep Daniel Safe. Nothing else mattered. Something as random as a cold could mean a trip to the emergency room and so we learned to avoid anyone who was sick. Things like mould, dust, and cold weather could initiate or worsen his asthma. When Daniel was around two-and-a-half years old, I kissed him after I'd eaten a piece of toast with peanut butter. Almost instantly a rash appeared on his cheek, and I realized then that he must be allergic to peanut butter. Daniel's skin tests confirmed that he was allergic to all nut products, along with his allergies to trees, plants, animals, dairy products, and eggs. The egg allergy meant he couldn't get normal vaccinations because of the underlying risk of an anaphylactic reaction to egg protein found in childhood vaccinations.

I was six months pregnant with our daughter, Aimee, during one of Daniel's worst asthmatic attacks. We took him to Etobicoke General Hospital, where our physician met us. Daniel was admitted shortly after we arrived.

On the pediatric floor of the hospital, a kind young nurse took Daniel's hand and pricked it with a needle and then she attached an IV drip. Prednisone began coursing through his tiny veins. Bruce and I decided that I would stay with Daniel overnight and he would come back in the morning.

"Call me if anything changes. There's a lounge at the end of the hall. Why don't you go down there? You might be able to get some rest," Bruce said.

"I can't sleep knowing Daniel is hooked up to all of this," I said, pointing to the IV drip. "I'll stay in his room. I'll be okay. Love you." I blew him a kiss.

After Bruce left, I created a makeshift bed with two chairs, and some extra blankets and a pillow that I had found in the linen closet. An older nurse walked into Daniel's room. "Mrs. Keane, your son will be fine. Try not to worry. We would like to put him in a croup tent tonight. I didn't want to alarm you if you walked in and saw the tent in his room."

"Will he be in the croup tent all night?"

"Yes, it will be good for him. And one of the nurses on duty in the morning will show you how to massage his back. Gentle massage helps to clear the mucus in the lungs."

"I didn't know that."

"The tea is in our staff room beside the nurses' station. And just in case you can't sleep (she knows that I will not sleep through the night) please feel free to use our library. We have a shelf packed with information on asthma, and how to help manage your child's disease." The word disease stuck in my mind.

"Thank you. I'll take a look."

"Your son will be fine."

After the nurse left, I began planning the rest of my night. *First, I'll make sure Daniel is fine and then I'll sleep for a few hours. Then I'm going into that library and read. Learn all I can about asthma.* That very long night gave me hope. Sitting in the narrow nurses' staff room lined with bookshelves, I realized that I had the power to keep my son safe. Knowledge is what I needed. I read until six a.m. and went back down the hall to see Daniel standing in the hospital crib with his big smile, completely charming the nurses.

"Good morning," I chirped, picking up Daniel. "I'm Daniel's mom. Do you think you could show me how to massage my son's back?"

After a few days Daniel's breathing improved. Soon he was feeling better and running up and down the halls near his room while the nurses chased him. Catching his little hand, a nurse hoisted him into her arms en route to the lab for blood work and more tests.

When Aimee was born in June of 1988, Daniel's asthma was under control, and he now had a sister, a playmate, and a friend. Our lives settled into the simple routines of raising children, along with the occasional visit to the emergency room. While I felt more confident about looking after my son and daughter, I was facing the daily challenges of parenting largely on my own.

Bruce was busy growing his manufacturing business, and that meant that he travelled extensively selling his products. During this time I was developing an autoimmune condition myself: Ankylosing spondylitis (AS). AS is an arthritic condition that causes pain and stiffness throughout the body—in my case, inflammation of the spine. The disease left me drained, but it would be many more years before I had an actual diagnosis of the condition. I began feeling isolated in our home on the outskirts of Milton. I wonder sometimes if our son felt the weight of my loneliness and anxiety, especially when he was sick.

Daniel's asthma was now compounded by anaphylaxis (food allergies). When Daniel was six he attended elementary school in Milton. After putting him on the bus, I'd walk with Aimee to her school down the road. When I came back home I began cleaning up the entire house, even the rooms that didn't require my attention. Staying busy kept me from thinking about Daniel, in a large school with children who ate peanut butter. Then, right before noon most days, I'd begin staring at the clock in the kitchen, afraid that someone from his school would call and tell me that Daniel had come in contact with peanut butter.

"Please come to the school. Daniel's had an allergic reaction."

During Daniel's first year away from me, I lived in fear that some food allergen would send him into an anaphylactic shock. Having asthma increased the risk of sudden death from an allergic reaction. The body's autoimmune system reacts to the offending allergen (peanut butter) by attacking itself. Major organs respond by shutting down. I had done what I could to prepare Daniel for entering elementary school, including sticking out-of-date EpiPens into grapefruits to show teachers what to do. The auto-injector syringes that Daniel carried contained a fast-acting dose of epinephrine and could be self-administered. I spoke at school assemblies, hoping my information would bring awareness, and hosted support meetings in our home for other parents who had children with food allergies.

My next line of defense was to become a volunteer at his school. Helping children learn to read aloud was rewarding. However, the bonus was that it allowed me to be near Daniel.

In the early nineties there was no public awareness around life-threatening food allergies. Our family learned to live with anaphylaxis, but communicating the risks to others was still a daily challenge.

"Even ingesting the smallest amount of nuts, dairy, or egg could result in a fatal anaphylactic reaction for my son," I repeatedly told teachers and school officials until someone finally listened to me.

One day I made a phone call to the superintendent of our school board. I was pleased by his willingness to be supportive.

"If you can put together a presentation regarding anaphylaxis, and demonstrate to our principals the adverse risk of having peanut butter in our classrooms, well then, I think we have a chance of banning the product in our schools," he said.

I contacted Daniel's allergist, who agreed to speak to the school administration along with me. Shortly after our presentation, peanut butter was banned in Halton

Separate School Board elementary schools. Naturally, there were parents who were against the peanut butter ban and felt that their rights had been taken away, but in the end, there was enough support from the community and administrators. Although Daniel still had to carry his EpiPens with him everywhere he went, I was comforted by the fact that peanut butter was not going to be anywhere near our son at school.

On March 14, 1994 our third child, Emily, was born. We were now a family of five.

Chapter Three

Photo Album

Oakville, December 15, 2011

I had been avoiding the worn-out blue photo album that lies in wait for me every day. Seeing the photo album stacked on top of a bunch of books in the room where I write makes me feel miserable. But on this day I opened the photo album and began to absorb myself in our old life.

The photos in the album were taken long before digital technology. Under a clear film sheet are photographs of my son, Daniel, the leading man in the film loop that is forming in my brain. Audioslave's *I Am the Highway* provides the soundtrack in my mind. The gritty lyrics describe the agony of someone being left behind.

As I turn the pages of the photo album, fresh images of Daniel pass in front of me.

A newborn baby asleep in my arms as I walk along the beaches in Toronto. In Mexico, Daniel and his dad by the hotel pool: his dad stands behind ready to catch him if he falls. A two-year-old Daniel sitting on his dad's lap, clapping hands and smiling as his mom takes the picture.

On another page Daniel is five years old, wearing a denim shirt. He tips his head to one side and grins for the camera. His mischievous smile exposes his baby teeth; his wavy dark brown hair is cut short.

Daniel developed physically at a slower rate than other kids because he had to avoid so many foods. In some of these photographs, I notice that his belt is tightly cinched around his slender waist so that his pants don't fall down.

On a summer day Daniel is riding his bike on a neighbor's laneway. His hair is unruly as he races by me. Not a care in his world.

Flipping to the next page, I look at a photograph of Bruce teaching Daniel how to drive a boat. He is seven in the photograph and wearing his dad's 1990s oversized sunglasses; he grips the steering wheel with two hands, yelling: "Put the hammer down, daddy!"

I'm in a time warp, but now that I've opened the album I can't stop myself from looking at the photographs. The heavy metal sounds of Pink Floyd's *Comfortably Numb*, my son's music, throb in my head as I wander through our good life.

As Daniel grew up he experimented with shaving his wavy hair. But the smile remained. The movie of Daniel and his sisters growing up continues as I turn another page. I find a photograph of Daniel and Aimee at Halloween. The picture was taken a long time ago. Aimee wears pink ballerina shoes as she leans on me, sitting on the couch in Milton. Daniel stands beside me, wearing a pirate's costume from the dollar store. A black patch covers his right eye. Another picture shows Daniel waving to the camera as he waterskis on our bay at the cottage.

I am reminded that Daniel taught himself to water-ski and wakeboard. Sometimes when he was skiing he'd take one foot out of the ski boot and dangle his other foot in the fast-moving wake, mostly just for fun and to get a reaction from whoever was spotting him.

In another shot, Daniel is at the cottage. He is nine and about to throw a tennis ball in my direction. It appears that he is also trash talking me. Why? I am not sure. I know it was cold outside because long icicles have formed above the front door. Daniel's hair is matted from wearing his winter hat.

And then there's Emily as a toddler. Daniel is kneeling beside her as she plays with her blocks. He is wearing a Toronto Maple Leafs sweater, with a big white C sewn onto the front of his jersey. He smiles.

Near the end of the album I find photographs of Daniel and his dad on a holiday in Puerto Rico. They are shaking hands after playing a round of golf. He comes up to his dad's shoulders in this shot. I notice that his smile has changed. His braces made him self-conscious. He wears one of his dad's golf shirts, and a leather belt that holds up his long Bermuda shorts.

Then there is a photograph of our three kids. We were catching the sunset. Daniel wears his ball cap in the backwards way young guys do, but even with his mouth full of braces he has a huge smile for me. His sisters smile too as they nudge close to him.

On the last pages of the photo album I notice that Daniel has physically matured.

He is taller and his legs and arms are muscular. There is a staged photograph of our family at the cottage during a Thanksgiving weekend. The photographer has managed to get all of us onto one red Muskoka chair. We're squished like sardines, but we don't care because we have the whole weekend ahead of us. Daniel and his dad are anxious to be done with the photography session so they can play golf. The backdrop of the photograph looks like a Tom Thompson painting, all fallen red and gold leaves and birch bark covering the ground.

And then I see Daniel as a young man. Shooting a puck on a makeshift rink on the lake. Sitting on the dock on a summer day, he strikes the pose of Rodin's *Thinker*. He is wearing his burgundy rash-guard shirt, waiting to go wakeboarding. His hair is cut short so there is no hint of his wavy hair. I can't tell if he was actually in deep thought or posing for the camera. His big grin has created deep lines on both sides of his mouth. Our son laughed a lot.

Here's Daniel at the finals of a track meet in grade twelve. He is the lead runner of the 4 x 100 relay. He stands on the track holding the baton scratching his chin while another runner walks into his sightline. Daniel stares straight ahead. He is focusing on the race, which was about to begin.

On the very last page of the album, we are at Daniel's graduation from high school. He is wearing a dark blue gown. The world was his for the taking. Isn't that what we said to him on his graduation day? We were all happy for Daniel, and very proud too. I felt relief that day. Daniel had made it through high school despite my worries about his food allergies. He was going to attend university in the fall. Daniel was in control of his destiny.

Daniel had grown up between the pages of the old blue photo album. Physically, he was a different person from the little boy looking at me in the first few pages. He was still my fun-loving, mischievous son, but the awkwardness and self-consciousness of his early teens had evaporated. Replaced by confidence. The mole above his lip that mirrored mine is noticeable in the photographs, along with his hundred freckles. It was clear from our family photographs that Daniel had a sense of himself and what he wanted from life and I can see that in the photographs. He was also restless. Rather than teach you how to do something, he would rush ahead and do it for you, which meant that I was always asking him for help. I remember his temper, too, but mostly I remember his captivating smile. Shutting the photo album I think of *The End* by Pearl Jam. I hear Eddy Vedder's strained voice singing about lost dreams and abandoned plans.

Chapter Four

Tipping Point

Bonita Beach, Florida, January 2, 2012

On a warm winter morning, I have come back down to Florida to think about the point in time at which Daniel's life began to unravel. I have been searching for the moment when I could have seen changes in Daniel—changes whose significance I did not understand. I had no idea what was happening to my son.

That afternoon, I was having difficulty concentrating. Thoughts were not coming easily for me. Instead of writing I closed my notebook, grabbed my sunglasses, and went for a walk on the beach. Mounds of twisted plants and bark were scattered over the beach. But it wasn't just plant roots on the shore. Dead, rotting fish were also tangled in the seaweed. Their silvery, hollowed-out remains had been tossed onto the beach by the infamous Florida red tide. *What a mess*, I thought to myself. My refuge had become a graveyard.

The remains of the red tide were worse the farther north I walked. After seeing so many dead fish, I turned around and headed back to my spot on the beach.

Sitting down on the lounger, I rested my head on the

back of the chair, shut my eyes; soon thoughts of Daniel filled my mind. Possible reasons for *why* knitted together. I began to have a sense of clarity, which allowed me to begin the process of understanding why everything went so terribly wrong.

. . . .

Oakville, March 10, 2006
During the winter of 2006 I had felt run-down. Flat-out exhausted even after a short run. The joint pain was constant. And to make things worse I was training for a spring marathon. On one of my long training runs from Oakville to Burlington and back again (30 kilometers) I started feeling pain in my stomach; and then the diarrhea started. I stopped running. But knowing that I had no choice if I was to make it home I started running (slowly) again. I felt humiliated as I crawled my way back to Oakville. That day, I was beginning my own struggle with a second debilitating disease, a condition that would leave me less time to think about Daniel. And perhaps that's part of the reason I misread signs that must have been there.

Finally, after months of bleeding and bouts of painful diarrhea, tests revealed that I had Ulcerative Colitis: one of the inflammatory bowel diseases. More tests would confirm that I had also suffered for years with Ankylosing Spondylitis: inflammation of the spine. The inflammation was painful, and stress made the condition worse.

Oakville, May 20, 2006
As the spring months unfolded, Bruce and I would of-

ten talk about our plans for the upcoming summer at our cottage.

"Go up north and rest. I'll try to get up on Thursdays when I can," Bruce said.

"I'm looking forward to the summer. Hanging out with the kids. Catching the sunset. The last time that I felt so tired was when we were in Milton and the kids were young."

"You'll enjoy having Daniel around after his first year away."

I didn't share my health challenges with Daniel until we were both at the cottage that summer. And when I finally did, he encouraged me to stop running. My ability to persevere was not lost on my son. That summer when he realized that I had left the cottage and gone for a run he would often follow me in his truck. Coming to my rescue, he'd roll down the window and say, "Mom, why are you doing this to yourself? C'mon, get in the truck and I'll take you back to the cottage."

"Daniel, I have to do something. I can't sit around all day."

"You're supposed to be taking it easy."

"I know dear, you're right."

I got into Daniel's truck thankful that he followed me.

Daniel was back at the cottage after his first year at the University of Ottawa. He was in his sixth year working at the Silver Stream Farms market in Port Sandfield. He had taken pride in becoming the manager of the produce department, the focal point of the store. Celebrities and hockey players who summered in Muskoka often came in and chatted with Daniel. Our son was hardworking and friendly. That summer, however, he managed to keep up his genial disposition only at work. At the cottage he was remote and irritable. He was not happy.

Instead of coming home and calling out for someone to drive the boat so he could wakeboard, he came in the door, grabbed something to eat, and fell asleep in front of the television.

"How was your day at the store?" I'd ask.

"All right, Mom, I'm really tired. When do you think dinner will be ready? I'm gonna sleep for a few hours."

"Why do you have to be at the store so early in the morning?"

"'Cause, they open at eight now. The fruits and vegetables have to be sorted and washed earlier and I have to make sure that the guys in produce are doing their job."

"Get some rest," I offered.

Some days during that summer Daniel would go into his room and not come out for hours. He was physically exhausted, but he was also distant from us. This was also the first summer that Daniel began going out with his friends to the bars in Port Carling.

· · · ·

Bonita Beach, Florida, January 2, 2012
An hour later I looked up from my rambling notes and saw that the beach was now packed with children and parents. Reluctantly, I returned to my memories.

During the summer of 2006 Daniel and I didn't have a lot of time to talk about his first year at university. He was growing up and I had to cut the maternal strings. But I misread his fatigue and agitation. I assumed that it was a result of his late-night drinking, and having to get up early for work. Before that summer, I would have described our life at the cottage as Utopian. I had slipped into thinking that our family was healthy. And I believed that even with the mounting pressures of school and work, we would always manage to find our way to the cottage to be together. In the spring of that year, Daniel had talked about leaving the market and looking for a job in the city.

"I might apply to some banks or accounting firms this summer. Maybe work in Toronto. Get some experience in the financial industry. I don't know. I'm not that interested in going back to the store," he said.

"Great idea, Daniel," Bruce said. "Maybe consider applying at smaller firms where you would get a broader introduction to running a business. Expose yourself to sales, customer service, even marketing."

"Yeah. Makes sense."

"Maybe working in a corporate setting will help you decide on some of your second-year courses."

"I'll see what's out there."

But in May, one of the owners of Silver Stream Farms made an offer that Daniel couldn't turn down. The money, along with the idea of being up north again for the summer, was too good to pass up. Quietly, I was thankful that we could be together again at our cottage for the summer.

One afternoon in July when we had time to talk, I asked Daniel what courses he was planning to take in second year. He then admitted that he had been asked to leave the International Business program in Ottawa. I was stunned.

"Why didn't you tell me that you were kicked out of your program?"

"I didn't completely fail the year. I got some of my credits. They asked me to consider another program, but I don't want to go back to Ottawa."

He saw the shocked look on my face.

"I should have taken the year to work," he added. He assumed, because it had been his decision to attend Ottawa U, that he couldn't tell us how much he hated being there, or that he was failing his year. Instead of drilling down to determine why Daniel had done poorly at school my solution was to fix the problem. But the problem was so much deeper than being asked to leave his program.

"I knew you and Dad would be upset with me. I didn't tell you because I wasn't ready to deal with it. I wanted to forget about it."

"Daniel, what went on in Ottawa? Was it drinking, drugs?" I asked. "I did pot."

He continued. "Look, Mom, I'm telling you this because I want you to understand what was going on. Sometimes we went over to Hull because we could get into the bars. One night, my buddies and I left a bar and were just walking down the street. These guys came out behind us and one of them said my friend was hitting on his girlfriend. Then he punched my friend in the head."

"What did you do?"

"I grabbed the guy and took him off my buddy. It got too crazy, so we stopped going over."

"Is that the reason why you were asked to leave your program in Ottawa? Was it because you chose to party instead of doing the work? You were lucky you didn't get hurt."

"I did, Mom, I just never told you."

I told Daniel that he would have to tell his dad what had happened in Ottawa, and although I was disturbed by his behaviour, I felt that he had put that experience behind him and was interested in a fresh start at another university in the fall. Daniel called his dad from the cottage later that day and explained the situation. To his credit, Bruce handled the news better than I thought. Still, he was disappointed that his son had kept this to himself. For the rest of the month of July we put our energy into helping Daniel find a new school. After many calls and letters of support for our son, Daniel was accepted into the Communications program at Laurier, in Kitchener-Waterloo. I imagined then that some of Daniel's malaise was attributable to being ousted from his program in Ottawa. He kept all of it inside, afraid to tell us the truth. But why did I have to drag the information out of him? What was at the root of our son's behavioural changes in his first year at university?

Then, on a beautiful summer day in 2006, our family contentment took another jolt. The day started with our morning routines: breakfast, and then the kids going off to summer jobs. By then, Daniel had left the market and was working at the LCBO in Port Carling and The Rock Golf Course in Minett. Daniel's new jobs seemed to energize him.

That evening, Daniel's sisters and his cousin Jacqueline and I sat in the screen porch having dinner, enjoying the warmth of the summer night. The sunlight glittered on the water near our dock. An industrious hummingbird perched by the window of the screen porch sucking the sugary mixture from the feeder. After our meal we cleaned up the kitchen and put away the leftovers. Daniel excused himself and went into his room.

A few hours later I looked in on him. He was in a deep sleep and snoring loudly, so I assumed he would be in for the night.

Later on, the girls watched a movie and then went to their rooms, because both Aimee and Emily had to be up early the next day for work. I decided to go to my bedroom to read. Just after ten o'clock Daniel opened his bedroom door and walked down to my room. I was sitting up in bed. I set my book down when I saw Daniel in the doorway wiping his eyes and yawning.

"What time is it, Mom?"

"Ten after ten," I said.

"Are you okay if I go over to Newton's tonight? Pete is having some friends over at his boathouse."

I hesitated and looked over my shoulder at the clock sitting on the bedside table. It was the beginning of the summer and Daniel and I had already had a number of conversations about going out to bars and drinking, and then coming home in the middle of the night and relying on coffee and energy drinks to stay awake the next day. He saw the pained expression on my face.

"Don't worry so much, Mom. I am going to grab a flashlight and walk over to Pete's. He has a bunch of the guys over that I haven't seen since last fall."

That summer at the cottage I had begun to notice a change in Daniel. Usually, he was the cheerleader, getting his family motivated to do things like water ski or cruise the lakes. That July he was less interested in doing the things that we had done as a family.

And the long hours at work and the late nights partying were catching up to him.

He was often irritable, particularly in the morning. He seemed constantly stressed, pissed off at the world.

"Daniel, I know that you want to see your friends, but you're spending a lot of time and money at the bars up here. It's not a healthy lifestyle, and you're obviously exhausted from working all day and staying up so late."

"C'mon. I've been on my own all year. I can look after myself."

"I am not going to get into an argument with you tonight. Yes, you're an adult. But it is my job as your mother to intervene when I think you're doing something harmful."

"What do you mean?"

"All I'm saying is, you have to get up very early every morning for work. Staying out late partying is not something you have done in the past. At least, when you lived at home. You've always been responsible. What has changed?"

"Nothing. I just want to hang out with my friends tonight."

"Promise me you'll come home at a reasonable time."

"I will."

"Take your key, and lock the front door when you leave, okay? See you in the morning. Love you." I replied.

Daniel walked over to my side of the bed and gave me a hug, something he always did when he was going out.

"Love you too, Mom. Don't worry about me so much. I'm fine. 'Night."

"Goodnight dear."

I nodded off in bed waiting for Daniel to come home. When I woke up and looked over at my clock it was three-thirty in the morning. My first thought was that Daniel had not come home from the party at the neighbour's boathouse. I didn't remember hearing the key in the lock; I always heard that telltale sound when Daniel or Aimee were out at night.

Damn it! Didn't we just have this conversation about staying out all night? He promised that he would be home in time to get a decent sleep.

I got out of bed and walked down the hall to Daniel's room. Opening the door I still held out hope that he had slipped into bed quietly. But he wasn't there. I immediately felt that familiar pang of protective worry mixed with anger. I wasn't sure what to do. I left his room and opened the glass door that overlooks the bay. I swung it wide open and instantly heard the sounds of people jumping off of the boathouse and screaming as they hit the water. The party had degenerated into an alcohol-soaked binge. This was dangerous. Then I thought about Daniel. Where was he?

Pete's parents were on a canoe trip, and his friends had taken over the cottage and boathouse. I slammed the door shut and picked up the phone. I tried calling their cottage. Whoever answered the phone was wasted. I hung up and called Daniel's cell phone. Blood pounded in my ears as nightmarish scenarios replaced rational thoughts.

Had Daniel drunk so much that he'd blacked out? Was he floating face down in the bay? I was stricken with terror. Daniel finally answered his cell phone.

"Yeah. Who is this?"

"It's your mom! Daniel, get home now!"

"What's the matter, Mom? Why are you so angry?"

"You're drunk; that's why I'm so angry. Get home right now!"

My son was incoherent. I hung up the phone and wandered back to my room, and turned the radio on. I lay waiting to hear the latch click in the door. This was so completely out of his character.

When Daniel did come home it was well after four a.m. I had never been in a situation like this and I knew there would be no reasoning with him in his condition.

I heard him fumbling around in the dark, bumping into walls, and then he found his bedroom door. After turning on the light he shut his door and fell into bed. I exhaled some of the anxiety that had been building that evening. I was boiling mad at my son, for this night and all the other nights I had worried about him. But this evening had been the worst. Clearly, he'd had too much to drink, and he was not at all remorseful. As his mother, I felt I had no choice but to confront him, even in the messed-up state we were both in.

Walking down the hallway to his room, I tugged the girls' bedroom doors shut. My niece was staying with us, and I didn't want anybody to see Daniel like this. At the end of the hallway I stood in front of my son's room and thought about what I would say to him. Then I knocked on his door and gently nudged it open. Daniel slowly rolled over to see who was standing in his room. A piece of his bed sheet stuck to the side of his face. As he got up, the sheet peeled off of his face and fell to the bed. He had managed to put on pajama bottoms, but his slim, muscular torso was exposed. He walked toward me angrily, as if he thought I was invading his space. His eyes were like little crystals, glassy and bloodshot. The odor of stale beer lingered on his breath.

"Daniel, what are you doing with your life?" I said.

"What's wrong?" he asked in a slurred voice. "Why are you so mad at me?"

Frustration and fear were bubbling up inside, and in that moment I was scared for Daniel. Standing in his room, my son felt like a stranger; he was going through a transformation I didn't want to see.

"What were you doing over at Newton's? I could hear all of you yelling and carrying on, and you're all drunk! People jumping off the diving board! Someone is going to get hurt."

Daniel moved closer to me and said: " You don't know what you're talking about. Get out of my room so I can sleep."

"Don't talk to me that way. I can't sleep, wondering if you're safe. Worrying that you've been involved in an accident, always on guard at night thinking that something terrible has happened to you, and you don't care."

Daniel stood in front of me, and with both hands pushed me out of his room and into the hallway. I was stunned that my son had physically removed me from his room; Daniel had crossed a line. What had I done to deserve such contempt? I lashed out at him.

"You're drinking way too much. You're risking your life. We need to deal with whatever's causing you to lose control. This impulsive behaviour is upsetting to your sisters. Daniel, they look up to you."

Daniel leaned on the wall beside the door in his bedroom, staring into my eyes as I kept up my tirade. "You seem so agitated, lately. I am not going to sit by while you ruin your life."

I walked back to my bedroom. Daniel shut his door and fell asleep on his bed. His behaviour that night revealed more than I could comprehend at the time. His actions were a call for help. None of us understood that Daniel was in the depths of a major depression.

The commotion in the early hours of the morning between Daniel and me had woken the girls. Emily and her cousin peered into the hallway. I told them to go back to bed.

I picked up the phone to call Bruce, and then I hesitated. I didn't want to wake him, but I was frightened. A moment later I was calling Oakville.

"Bruce, you have to come up to the cottage as soon as you can," I said, sobbing into the receiver. "Daniel came home drunk. He was banging into walls. Then we got into an argument and he pushed me out of his room. It was awful, and I don't know what to do. This is not the son we know. What's happening to Daniel?"

"What! Lynn. Where is Daniel right now?"

"He is in his room, asleep."

"I'll drive up tomorrow morning. Let Daniel know that I will be there around noon."

"Bruce, I'm afraid. Daniel was full of rage. He needs help."

"Try to get some sleep," Bruce offered.

I put my head down on the pillow and cried. The bond between Daniel and me had been bruised. I hardly recognized the bitter young man in front of me tonight. It was clear I couldn't provide the help he needed. I had no idea what lay at the core of his pain.

"The next afternoon Bruce and I sat with our son in the screened porch at our cottage. Bruce was across from Daniel, his hands trembling as he spoke.

"You can't go on like this, Daniel. What's happening with you?"

"I don't know, Dad."

Our son looked awful. His skin was pale; there were dark circles under his bloodshot eyes. What had happened to him?

"Your mother stayed awake last night, worrying about you. And this wasn't the first time."

Clearing his throat, Daniel replied, "I'm sorry. I just wanted to have a good time with my buddies. I'm sorry I pushed you, Mom."

I kept my eyes on Daniel as he stared down at the grey floorboards, willing him to look up and tell me what was happening in his life.

Tears dripping down his cheeks, Daniel finally looked at his father. I wanted to let him know that he was loved and that he was a good son, in spite of what had happened the night before.

For the first time in Daniel's life I wasn't able to make everything better. How could I possibly fix what I couldn't see or understand?

"Daniel," Bruce said, "we love you and we will do everything to help you. But we need to understand what's going on in your life. I know it's hard trying to manage two summer jobs. What if you quit one? What about just working at the golf course?"

"Dad, you can't help me," Daniel replied, "I have to work this out on my own. I know I can't drink like that anymore. John (Newton) told me this morning that someone could have died with the amount of beer and liquor that was consumed last night."

"Daniel," I said, "drinking like that…"

"Mom, I know, I have to control myself."

Bruce was frustrated with Daniel's attitude.

"Son, it's black and white. You can't drink at all. It changes you. I don't want to ever see you end up like some of the guys I went to high school with. The drinking stops now!"

"Dad, I get it."

Daniel stood up and walked toward me. He apologized again for his actions. I held out my arms to hug him, feeling his tears as they ran down his face.

He walked over and hugged his dad. After the chaos of the previous evening we were all tired and scared.

Daniel, Muskoka, July 2006
John came looking for me after he got home from his canoe trip. He told me that I was lucky. He said the amount of alcohol that we consumed could have killed somebody. He scared the shit out of me, and I have never forgotten our conversation. He was calm, and I knew he was right. I have never felt so hung-over as I did that day. Maybe it's easier hearing about something stupid you've done from someone who is not your parent.

A thunderous summer storm broke the silence on the porch as the three of us sat there, not knowing who we should call for help. Large chunks of hail and heavy rain pelted down around us.

That afternoon, the storm churned up the water, producing long rolling waves that crashed onto the shore.

The drama of the summer storm momentarily took my mind off of our problems. I was thankful for the cool air that blew in from the bay.

I repeated my concern. "Dear, you need support. Someone you feel comfortable with, who can try to help you work through this. What if I call our family doctor and see if he can refer you to a therapist?"

"I don't want to talk to anyone, Mom. I'll deal with my problems on my own. I won't drink anymore. I'm done with it."

Although Daniel said he didn't want a therapist, I reached out for support and was surprised by the response I received:

"Your son will have to make the call to get help. He has to feel that he has hit bottom. He has to want help, so just keep encouraging him to seek support."

"Please call our family doctor," I said again and again to Daniel. But that is all I did.

I know now that Daniel was not functioning emotionally and was unable to ask for the support he needed.

That afternoon Daniel told us that his former boss at Silver Stream Farms had offered to let him stay in one of the apartments near the store in Port Sandfield.

"It will be better, Mom. And you won't have to worry so much about me."

I felt like I had been kicked in the stomach. Daniel had begun to think that our family would be better off without him around. I pleaded with him to stay.

"We have to work through this together," I said.

By the end of our conversation that afternoon, Daniel agreed to stay. We would pull together as a family. That's what families do. And although Daniel agreed to stay at our cottage and stop drinking, I was torn inside. Our tight-knit family tapestry was unraveling.

The day of reckoning on the porch was also the day that Daniel had the morning and afternoon shifts at the golf course, cleaning carts and dumping garbage bins in order to get the club ready for golfers the next day. He was hung over and emotionally drained, but determined that he would finish his shift. After he went to work, Bruce and I went for a long walk to try to figure out how to help our son.

Walking down the dusty road with our dog, Bailey, we talked about trying to engage Daniel again in the things he used to enjoy. Bruce would spend more time with him at the cottage, and I would continue to talk with him about what was going on in his life and at school. We would be there to support our son.

. . . .

Bonita Beach, Florida, January 2, 2012

More families have returned to the beach where I sit writing about Daniel. I watch as a little girl with blonde ponytails reaches up to grasp her father's hand. He cups his daughter's tiny fingers in his large palm. She follows him with her eyes. In unison they drop down to their knees and joyfully begin digging in the sand. I can't stop watching them.

As the sun dips behind the clouds, I feel a chill from the cool onshore breeze.

Leaning back on my beach chair, I spread my wrap over my bare shoulders, so I can stay a little longer on the beach and think about our son.

Chapter Five

Daniel and the Cottage

In 1991, with two kids in tow, we bought our cottage on Riverdale Road near Minett, in Muskoka. Emily, our third child, has never known a life that doesn't include going up north for the summer. Bruce and I always imagined that our small A-frame cottage, surrounded by hemlock and jack pine, would be a gathering place for the family.

I get nostalgic thinking about the cottage because so much of our family history was made there. And we have lived there longer than any other place, so we considered it our family home. It was Daniel's real home too, the refuge where he could be his essential self.

Daniel, Muskoka, May 15, 2007
I'm stoked. Starting my own business this summer. Going to hire a couple of friends and see if I can find a few guys up here who can work for me.

During the spring of 2007 Daniel and his dad had spent many hours preparing for his presentation to the Ministry of Development and Innovation, which grants funding through the Muskoka Small Business Summer Company Program to students who want to start a business in the Muskoka area during the summer months.

The previous winter we'd sat around the kitchen table discussing Daniel's ideas about starting a cottage maintenance business. He would also fill clients' boats and trucks with gas, and stock their fridges and bars. And he hoped that his passion for cooking would come in handy if a client wanted an event catered. Cottage Concierge would be a one-stop shop for cottage owners.

"Dad, hey. What's up?"

"Hi, Daniel. Are you on your way to Bracebridge right now?"

"Yeah, I'm feeling good about my business plan. Thanks for helping me put it all together."

"You're welcome, Daniel. Call me after you've made your presentation. I want to hear all about it."

"Board members from the region will be hearing our proposals too."

"Daniel, you've put a lot of effort into developing a strategy for CC. They'll see that. Be proud of what you've done," Bruce said.

"Okay, Dad, talk later."

As Daniel drove into Bracebridge for his presentation he thought about his dad and the hours the two of them spent working together on CC. He thought about the business articles that his dad had given him to read. He was confident. After a few rough years between his dad and him, Daniel sensed their relationship had changed for the better.

After Daniel delivered his presentation he drove back to Oakville. Walking in the door, he yelled out to me.

"Hey, Ma, where are you?"

I could tell by his tone that his presentation had gone well.

"Daniel, how did you do?"

"Great. They really liked my business plan, and I got accepted into the program. $1500 to start up, and another $1500 if I continue Cottage Concierge 'til September."

"Daniel, that's excellent."

"Mom, it was really cool. I explained that my concept was unique, because I could offer so many services to my clients."

"What did they think of your slogan, 'Taking the work out of your weekend'?" I inquired.

"I think they liked it. A reporter from the Bracebridge Examiner is going to interview me about the business next week."

"Why don't we sit down later today and make a list of potential clients. I'm sure I can come up with some names and phone numbers."

"Okay, Mom. I'm going to call Dad and let him know how it went."

"Sounds good."

"What's for lunch?"

. . . .

Daniel, Muskoka, May 30, 2007
All my life my mom's had to protect me. She wants me to have a normal life.

Daniel understood that sudden death was a possibility with life-threatening food allergies. Eating out was not generally an option for him. And when he did eat out, he would have to worry about who had prepared his food. Did the food come in contact with milk or nuts? By the time he was a young adult he was tired of being reminded of the fact that he could die from something he ate. A girl giving him a kiss with peanut butter on her lips could send him into an anaphylactic shock.

. . . .

Daniel stopped wearing his Medic Alert bracelet in high school. He would leave his life-saving epinephrine in places like the truck, where the temperature would reach over 100 degrees in the summer, rendering them useless. Daniel was different from everyone else, even his family.

He would say to me: "Mom, stop worrying about me. I'm fine."

"But you need to know where your EpiPens are. And don't leave them in your truck, baking in the heat."

As he got older he hated having to watch everything that he touched or put into his mouth. I understood that.

He had become a fan of the Food Network in his late teens, and learned how to create fabulous dinners for his friends and family. We all encouraged his desire to become a chef. During the summer of 2006, Daniel and I started talking about his interest in attending a culinary arts program. But he was frustrated that his allergies would prevent him from working in a kitchen.

"I've looked into schools. No one is going to let me

work in a kitchen with my allergies. They wouldn't take the chance."

"We'll just keep trying, Daniel."

"Mom, think about it. I'm in the kitchen of a busy restaurant. I'd be asked to work with all kinds of foods and sauces (peanut sauce) nuts, eggs, seafood. And I couldn't do it."

. . . .

Daniel, Muskoka, June 10, 2007
My folks are more chilled this summer. I hate it when they'd get into arguments because of me. Even my mom with her health stuff doesn't seem to be so tired this summer.

Muskoka, June 29, 2007
"We're on the right side of summer," one of our neighbours, John, called as he dipped his paddle into the calm water midway between his dock and ours. Bruce and I laughed. So did our cottage neighbours, who had gathered on our dock to celebrate the July long weekend.

John Newton's family lived all year 'round on our bay, in a traditional Muskoka-style home that he had built. When we purchased our cottage on Riverdale Road, it was the Newtons—John, his wife, Pam, and his two kids, Peter and Valerie—we met first. Over the years, we have spent a lot of time together. During Thanksgiving weekends our whole family attended the Newton Invitational Golf Tournament and the accompanying potluck supper, along with other neighbours from the road. At Christmas we would gather in the Newtons' home for holiday readings and songs, enhanced by the roaring fire in the family room. There were always lots of kids around, but when they realized that we were going to begin the readings of English poetry and prose, they'd scramble out of the house and head down to the makeshift hockey rink on the lake.

That summer night in 2007, we gathered on our dock with Pam and John and some other close neighbours, all of us feeling mellow over the prospect of an endless Canadian summer. John wanted to know more about Daniel's new venture.

"Daniel is launching a cottage maintenance business this summer. He's calling it Cottage Concierge!" Bruce announced.

"That's great news! He'll enjoy being outside after all of the years working at the market," Pam said.

"So what type of maintenance projects will Daniel and his crew take on?" John inquired.

"He's decided to start with outdoor work, taking down brush, mowing lawns and painting, that sort of thing. I'm sure his crew will be up for anything though," I replied.

"Does Daniel have clients booked yet?" asked Sue Elms, our next-door neighbour and John's sister.

"He has a few from working at the store. Daniel tells me that he has been asked to cater a couple of golf tournaments this summer. He seems to have lots of ideas about his business and it's great to see him so happy. His biggest challenge will be to hold onto reliable staff," Bruce said.

That July evening, our talk turned to boats. John had grown up in Muskoka, so he was familiar with many of the area's old inboards that quietly cruised the lakes. These beautifully crafted old wooden boats were often handed down from generation to generation. He and Bruce shared a passion for them; they represented the early twentieth century of boating on the Muskoka Lakes. Several years before, John had facilitated the purchase of the *Mackenzie*, on behalf of Bruce. The varnished mahogany boat was built in 1937 in Port Carling, Ontario.

As the sun dipped behind the tree line, Daniel and Aimee joined our party on the dock.

"Congratulations on your new venture, Daniel. You'll have no shortage of work around here. Do you have your crew lined up yet?" John asked.

"Yeah, Ryan, my friend from school, will be working with me, but I'd like to find some guys who live up here. It's too hard to find housing for staff."

Daniel beamed as he spoke about his plans.

"I'm not too worried though; I've got a few leads."

"Val is working at a restaurant in town. But I think she has some extra time on her hands. If you're short on staff, give her a call," John said.

"Thanks, John. I sent Val a text last week and she says that she would be interested in doing some painting with us."

Daniel sat down with us and shared more thoughts on his new business.

"I've heard back from a few people who want me to come by this weekend and quote on work around their cottages."

"I'm happy to spread the word about your services too, Daniel. And if I hear of anyone looking for work I'll let you know," John said.

"Thanks, John."

John had always shown a genuine interest in Daniel and what was happening in his world. Daniel had known him most of his life.

Aimee got up from her chair and walked over to me.

"Mom, Daniel and I are going to Taps in Port Carling tonight, and I said I'd be the designated driver. Are you okay with that?"

"That's fine, dear. What time do you think you'll be home?"

Although I had reservations about her driving on winding cottage roads at night I had to trust that they would be fine.

"Probably around one, one-thirty," Daniel replied.

"Aim, just be careful, and watch out for deer."

Daniel and Aimee said goodnight to us and raced up the jagged granite steps to our cottage.

The sky was dark as John and Pam got into their canoe. After a few paddle strokes, John turned back towards us in his customary way and said, "Fare thee well, my friends."

We wished a goodnight to our next-door neighbours, Sue and John Elms, as we climbed the steps to our cottage.

Daniel, Muskoka July 1, 2007
In the summer the Newton's take off in their truck with a canoe on the roof, heading farther north when Muskoka gets jammed. John was a documentary filmmaker. He told me about his trip to Africa after he graduated from school and how that experience gave him a different perspective on what he wanted to do with his life.

The summer was packed for Daniel. When he had extra time in the day, he'd come through the door with some of his crew and announce that he was home:

"Hi Mom! Can you make me a sandwich? We're going wakeboarding."

"Sure. Do you want a BLT?"

"Thanks, Mom. And maybe chips and iced tea."

"Sure. Do you want me to make sandwiches for your crew?"

"That would be great. I'm going to get changed."

My eyes followed Daniel's back as he rushed down the hallway to his bedroom, and I couldn't help thinking how much progress he had made since the summer of 2006.

Daniel and his crew often worked long into the night completing projects for their clients. Cottage Concierge was becoming popular with cottagers in the area. The downside of this was that some of the crew would blow off a day here and there, or leave early with some excuse. And Daniel understood that his clients' satisfaction was key to his success with the business.

Daniel, Muskoka, August 24, 2007
Next year my buddy, Connor, will be staying here in Muskoka and he's going to come and work with me. Two guys I've hired this summer are jerks. They show up for their cheques, that's it. I can't depend on them to put in a full day's effort.

Regardless of who showed up for work Daniel would stay until the job was finished. Sometimes he would leave a job site at the end of the day to drive the guys to wherever they were staying, and then drive back to finish up himself. His work ethic and ethos did not go unnoticed. And as a result Daniel enjoyed long-standing relationships with his clients.

But in 2007 he had an experience with a client that would essentially wipe out his profits in his first year of business.

Daniel was owed thousands of dollars from a client for labour and materials. He hired a lawyer from Port Carling so that he could be represented in small claims court. A debt like this meant that Daniel would be behind in paying his crew and suppliers. It was a mess. Daniel couldn't focus on anything, and he fell behind with his Cottage Concierge paperwork.

By the end of the summer of 2007, Bruce had to step in and help pay some of the crew's wages. Even still, Daniel did not back down. He wanted what was owed to his company. By late fall, when Daniel was back at school, he realized that he didn't have the energy or resources to go after the client. Daniel was visibly stressed and he knew that he had no way now to recoup his loss.

Daniel, Muskoka, September 1, 2007
I left Laurier and now I'm at a community college. I have to deal with my insomnia, lying awake most of the night. I'm always exhausted. It's hard to focus on what's going on in the lectures. I have to get my credits and be done with school.

Daniel, Waterloo, September 15, 2007
I'm working at a store in the mall in Waterloo, making some extra cash and trying to keep up with my courses.

One weekend when he was home from school, during the fall of 2007, Bruce and Daniel agreed it was time to stop chasing the deadbeat client and move on.

"Daniel, look, you can't keep going after this guy. He has taken advantage of you. Accept the fact that he has no intention of paying you. It's a tough lesson."

"Dad, first I quoted a painting job at his cottage. Then he'd inspect what we did every day. Okay, cool, he wants a decent job. But then he and his wife kept asking us to do more. And I told him that my quote would change. He's like, 'That's fine. You guys are doing a good job.' By the time we finished at his place, my costs were way over what I had estimated. He knew he wasn't going to pay me and he let us continue working."

"You can't let this experience stop you from what you want to do with CC. You have to move forward. It's been a time-killer for you. Trust me. From now on you'll be more selective with new clients. And you will have to insist on a deposit which covers at least part of your materials and time."

"Yeah, Dad, you're right. Other tradespeople have been screwed by this guy too."

"I'm not surprised, Daniel."

Daniel, Waterloo, December 4, 2007

Alex and I started seeing each other. We met on the porch at Silver Stream. We realized we'd worked together at the store a long time ago. We talked about music. We both liked hip-hop and reggae. She's got this kind of natural thing about her. When she came to Waterloo to see me this fall we went to Starbucks and I had this amazing feeling with her. We talked a long time about our plans and our families. She told me about her dad and his challenges. I told her that I wanted to open a restaurant one day and live in a fragrant rustic log cabin, with a huge porch, and a kitchen that was safe and that I felt comfortable cooking in. She knows that I'm struggling keeping up with school, but she is super supportive.

Daniel, Oakville, December 17, 2007
Al's at McGill, in Montreal, so we're on our cell phones all the time. My dad asked me the other day who I was talking to so much because my cell phone bills were several pages long. "The charges are through the roof! You're going to have to start paying these phone bills," he said.

Daniel, Waterloo, January 25, 2008
This winter I started working for a guy named Gary. He does snow removal in Waterloo, and calls me in the middle of the night to plow his customers' driveways. Some nights if there's a ton of snow I call Mark, a buddy of mine, and we'll work most of the night together. Then I go back to my place and crash. The extra money helps out, especially right now. I can't believe my company did so well the first summer and this f—ing client basically wiped out any profits I made. If I can get CC going next summer, the way I manage the business will be very different.

Daniel, March 13, 2008
Lately, my folks are on me about not showing up on weekends. Especially when I tell them that I'll be home. I don't want my parents to see my emotional shit, so I say I have to stay, to work on school projects. That usually stops them from asking me to come home.

When I don't show up at the last minute I know it pisses them off, but there are days when I'm living in a dark, empty place and I don't want to be around anyone.

But when I'm feeling okay I'll go home. Many times my mom and I head to the grocery store to shop for stuff for a meal. We'll come back and hang out in the kitchen, just talking while I prep the food. When I'm cooking I've got the computer on and I'm checking the recipe. I'm like a juggler, keeping track of timing and ingredients, putting it all together. Creating a meal that everyone loves is the reward. Makes me feel good.

Daniel, Waterloo, March 28, 2008
Last time my mom drove me back to Waterloo, and we were listening to Pearl Jam's song, Black. I told her that Eddy Vedder wrote the lyrics about a friend of his who died. "She'll be a star in someone else's world." She tried to hide the fact that she was crying. Maybe the lyrics made her think of me.

Daniel, Muskoka, May 14, 2008
I've got one year of experience with CC, and some new projects lined up. I have two guys working for me this year, Connor and Sean, who are buggers. They're not afraid to work. And they'll do it as long and hard as me.

Daniel, Muskoka, June 16, 2008
"Anything I can do to help you with Cottage Concierge, dear?" she says.

This summer my mom brought up a large whiteboard and markers so I can keep track of all of the maintenance projects. I know she is trying to keep me organized, but this year I feel like I'm on top of things.

Daniel, Muskoka, June 21, 2008
*I'm at Adam's cottage. He and his wife want me to create a garden with plants that are native to Muskoka. The plan is to surround the front steps of their cottage with plants and shrubs, and then have it all spill down to the river. Alex is going to help me with the planting after I prep the gardens. The other day while I was at Adam's laying down sod, I saw a big motherf***** black bear. It stood up on its haunches—it was massive. I was surprised to see a bear that close to me. Going to go back to the cottage and grab something to eat and see if someone can take me for a ride (wakeboard).*

Muskoka, July 3, 2008
On Thursday July 3, 2008, while sitting on Sue's deck late in the day, I heard a loud thunderous bang, followed by a haunting silence. Within minutes, emergency sirens rang out all around the area. I guessed there had been a terrible car crash somewhere nearby.

After the noise and the frightening silence that followed I wanted to find my kids. When Sue came out of her cottage I yelled, "Did you hear a loud crash?"

"I thought it was a large truck going up our road," Sue responded.

Although we didn't know it then, out on the dark water of the bay, a catastrophic series of events was unfolding. Several boats from another marina were dispatched to the accident. There was a gap of time before we found out what had disrupted the tranquil summer day.

In times like this you do a mental inventory of where

your loved ones are, to see if they are safe. I knew Emily was at work at the market in Port Sanfield. She was fine, but where was Daniel? Then I remembered that he was working farther up on our road, clearing trees for a new landscape project. But I was still consumed with panic.

"Sue, I have to go. I need to find Daniel. I'm going to go back to my cottage. I'll see you later."

I tried to hide my terror. I turned and ran through the woods to my cottage. Racing up the back steps I met Aimee.

"Hon, did you hear a loud noise a few minutes ago?"

"No, Mom, I was in the shower. Do you want me to get in touch with Daniel and make sure he is all right?"

"Yes, dear!"

Aimee knew her mother well; she knew that I would not settle down until all of my kids were home safe. Aimee picked up the phone on the counter and called her brother.

"Hi, Daniel. Where are you?"

"I'm up on the road. What's up?"

"Can you come home?"

"Why, Aimee? What's going on?"

"There's been an accident. Mom thinks it's near the bridge on Peninsula Road."

"Okay, I'm finishing up anyway. I'll be home soon."

In a matter of minutes, inconceivable misfortune had struck several families, including one family who had a cottage not far from Riverdale Road. Never think that life is fair.

Aimee offered to pick up Emily; she would be done work soon.

"Wait, Aimee, I'll come with you."

The deafening sounds of the emergency vehicles on Peninsula Road made me hurry to catch up with her. The two of us hopped into my truck and backed out of the driveway and onto our cottage road, unsure of what we'd find.

Slowly winding our way to the bottom of the road we saw flashing lights at the entrance to Riverdale Road. There was already a lineup of vehicles trying to make the left-hand turn onto our road. A police officer directing traffic was stopping cars and making them turn around.

"Aim, stay here, they may have closed Peninsula Road. I'll walk down and see."

"Okay, Mom."

Aimee pulled my truck over to the side of our narrow cottage road.

As I walked down toward the highway, I had a sick feeling in my stomach, thinking about the silence that followed the loud crash. I thought of the rush of emergency responders fanning out around our bay. This had to be serious.

When I got to the end of our road, John Newton and some other neighbours were walking toward me. As they came closer, I could see the pained expressions on their faces. John left the group of men he was with and walked over to me.

"Lynn, I was talking to a volunteer fireman who was driving over the bridge and saw a car partly submerged in the water. He jumped off the bridge to help," he said. "A girl was able to get out and the paramedics were still working at the scene of the crash."

"Oh, John, that's terrible."

My neighbours and I walked back to my truck in shock. There was no "right side of summer" now.

I got back into the truck with Aimee and shared the details of what had happened by the bridge.

"I'll text Emily now. She's probably wondering what's going on too," Aimee said.

When the two of us got back to our cottage Daniel was home, waiting for us. We spoke briefly about what had happened. He offered to pick up his sister at the market.

After Daniel left, Aimee and I went down to the dock, trying to comprehend the tragedy on our bay. I thought of the families who would be going about their day. And then there would be a knock at their door, or a phone call that would change their lives forever. I thought about the mothers.

My neighbour, Sue, saw me sitting on my dock and came over.

"Did you hear from Daniel?"

"I did, Sue. He was working up the road. Thank God!"

Our dock was the gathering place that afternoon. We still didn't understand the scope of what was happening in real time. My focus had been on finding my kids. While we sat on our dock, a Boston whaler ferrying paramedics and one of the accident victims came racing toward the Joe River Marina, where the ambulances were standing by. My family and neighbours witnessed the shocking scene three times that day, knowing that each time it was a matter of life and death. A report from a newspaper article: *The OPP said its investigators had determined that alcohol and speed were definite factors in the crash. An autopsy confirmed that all three drowned.*

Time lost meaning for us as we remained on the dock that day. It was as if we were stuck in slow motion. I suggested that we make a potluck meal. Everyone went home and grabbed their leftovers and some wine and came back to our cottage. We spent the rest of the night sharing a community meal and being thankful. Staying together meant we could delay being alone with our thoughts and the events of a dreadful summer afternoon.

Throughout that summer we read newspaper accounts of the horrific details about the three young men who died in our bay. The *Toronto Star's* headline, "Music, laughter then dead silence," reminded me of the fragility of life. There is beauty and peace amid nature's magnificence. And then in an instant it can all be gone.

Over time the disturbing images slipped from our consciousness, but every time I drive by the crash site, thoughts of the accident in July of 2008 come back to me.

Everyone has a first day and a last day; the days in between are gifts.

A few weeks later, Daniel and I were talking about the accident on our bay. So much misinformation had leaked out; however, it was clear that drinking and speed had played a role. The accident had left three families without their sons, as well as a young woman who faced a lifetime of traumatic images and grief. The accident troubled Daniel. I suspect that he recalled his own excessive drinking. The tragedy was a sobering reminder.

I can see Daniel sitting on the edge of the fireplace while we chatted. His legs were smeared with paint from a client's project. He was wearing his trademark beige board shorts and one of his collection of vintage T-shirts that were threadbare and tight from being washed too many times. Daniel's hands were folded as he looked at me.

"I don't get it," he said.

"What do you mean?"

"It was senseless. The way those guys died."

He saw the danger that lurked in his reckless behaviour.

"There was a time when I did things, stupid things without thinking. Without caring about what could happen."

"We've had a lot of stress here the past few summers because of your drinking and impulsive behaviour."

"Yeah, I know, Mom, but I have moved on from that."

Daniel, Muskoka, July 18, 2008
Bad choices. I've made them too. But when you see the shit happening in front of you. Living for the moment. We make awful decisions we can't recover from.

During the summer and fall of 2008, Daniel was having the best time of his life. In two years he had matured and he also appeared to have direction in his life. His summer business, Cottage Concierge, was doing well and he had a long list of repeat clients. His spirits were lighter, too; gone was the edginess and the anger that had swept over him during the summer after his first year away at university. I remember thinking that this was the best summer for all of us in a very long time. The hypnotic warm days rolled into each other. And then the days became shorter, and the amount of sunlight washing over the dock grew less and less. Summer was winding down. Daniel would have been in an extended mania phase at this point in time. We had no idea.

Daniel, Muskoka, August 15, 2008
I feel bad that I broke up with Al by email. I knew she would be hurt, but I just couldn't face her. We had some great times together. I will always care about Al, 'cause she was there for me when things were not good in Waterloo. Her family was very good to me, too. I remember one night after I had finished a painting job, Al's parents invited me to dinner. Her sister took pictures of us sitting together on her deck, at sunset. In the shot white paint stains are all over my arms.

Daniel, Muskoka, October 11, 2008
The cottage will always be home for me. From the time I first came up here in 1991, when I was five years old, I would create all these outdoor adventures. One year, when we took the badminton net down, I made a few golf holes on the rocky slope next to the cottage.

Then the next year I made a dirt bike track for myself. I built snow forts on our old deck in winter and convinced my sisters to come and help me. Then we'd take snacks out to the fort and play board games. I was always outside, never wanted to come in.

On a late fall afternoon in 2008, the five of us were at our cottage to put away the last remnants of summer. The outdoor furniture had to be put away in the boathouse, and the eavestroughs had to be swept of debris and cleaned before the wet, cold November winds blew.

As I was making dinner in the cottage, I turned to see Daniel climbing a tall ladder on the deck, carrying a long green garden hose under his arm. Bruce stood adjacent to the ladder, which swayed precariously, as Daniel stepped on each rung. My first thought was to tell them to be careful, but I stopped myself. This was part of their fall ritual, so I went back to baste my turkey in the oven.

After an hour or so the two of them came into the cottage, shedding their sweatshirts and toques, and they ambled into the kitchen looking for something to eat.

"Smells amazing, Mom," Daniel pronounced.

After a snack, and a quick look at who was on top of the leaderboard in a golf tournament, they headed back out into the crisp air of the late fall day to finish their chores.

Bruce, with his *To Do* lists, and our son, content to do the physical labour.

Through the glass doors I watched as their work morphed into a great excuse to hang out together. I heard laughter and fragments of their conversations about golf and their latest football picks. Their breath forming wispy clouds above their heads as the light faded. As they worked away, I observed a father who loved his son more than he could express and a son who took great pleasure in being in his father's company.

Daniel, Waterloo, November 17, 2008
I want to tell my parents that some days I can't even pick up the phone to call them or anyone. I spend a lot of time on the Internet. Looking up recipes and lyrics, or searching some random fact. I'm sleeping more in the day; these

brutal sinus headaches make me feel sick.

A sense of not belonging was making Daniel feel alone and isolated in Waterloo. He was not attending school on any kind of regular basis. Anxiety and depression were closing in on him. He berated himself because he felt he hadn't lived up to what was expected of him, although everyone around him thought he was an accomplished young man. Daniel couldn't see beyond his failures and missed opportunities. He saw them as insurmountable problems, although his outlook stemmed from a change in his brain circuitry; it made him feel sad; it disconnected him from his family. No one around him understood why he was loaded with energy and ideas one minute, and then in the next, stressed and agitated. Daniel's relationships suffered from his sudden shifts in mood and behaviour. He began to spend more time away from friends and family; he stopped being able to share his problems, and he wasn't able to understand what was happening to his life. A vicious, deadly cycle that we should have seen for what it was: depression and mania, mania and depression.

Chapter Six

Spring

Daniel, Waterloo, St. Patrick's Day March 17, 2009
A few of my buddies, Connor, Shaun, and Ryan and I long boarded off a highway ramp in Waterloo to celebrate St. Patrick's Day this year. We had some great rides that day. Looking forward to getting to Muskoka this year. I'm feeling okay these days; maybe it's the light.

Daniel, Waterloo, April 3, 2009
My CC client Adam wants me to do more work for him this summer. He invited me to visit him in Toronto this past winter to see his construction projects. Maybe think about working for him at some point, but I didn't take him up on his offer. Right now I'm focused on making CC a full time operation. I know I have to tell my parents that I've left school. I will when I get the paperwork ready for CC's taxes.

In December of 2008 I seriously began wondering if Daniel was going to class. I'm not certain why. My worries felt random. At first, I kept these thoughts to myself, but in March of 2009 I brought the subject up with Bruce.

"I don't have anything really to base my concerns on, and maybe it doesn't make sense, but do you think Daniel is in school?"

"Why, Lynn?"

"I'm just unsure if he is actually in school. He calls me during the day when I think he should be in class. But when I question why he is not in class, he says that his class was cancelled or a prof didn't show up."

But I made excuses for my son's behaviour. Daniel was a great kid. He had never given us major cause to worry. I came across a card in my husband's office recently that illustrates our son's personality. It was a birthday card for Bruce's fifty-first birthday. In the card, each of us had written a few lines about celebrating life and hoping that 2009 would be "the best year ever." Daniel wrote about his dad's improving golf scores:

Happy Birthday Pops,
With the 2009 winter golf season rapidly approaching I would like to take this time to remind you that you are a "low handicapper" and I have a golf "handicap" thus an eight stroke minimum will be in effect during all the winter months. When spring arrives a recalculation will occur, also the added benefit of one more year under your belt makes you much wiser in all aspects of life but mainly "golf." Have a great year. 100-51 is 49.
You're on the good side of 50.
Love DK

Daniel, Oakville, April 12, 2009
I had another terrorizing nightmare last night. Some crazy dude was running after me. My heart was pounding.

I couldn't breathe because I was running so fast. The guy had a weapon that he was holding in the air as he ran after me. I woke up in a cold sweat. I can't get back to sleep after some of these dreams. The next morning I told my mom about it. She was getting something out of the fridge as we were talking. She shut the fridge door and sat down beside me. She said, "Daniel, that is awful. Does this happen often? Maybe you shouldn't watch such violent television shows." I don't know, maybe she's right. As we ate breakfast, we continued talking about my insomnia, but I don't think my mom understands how intense the nightmares can be and how they're messing with my sleep.

Separation

The real troubles in your life are apt to be things that never crossed your worried mind; the kind that blind-side you at four p.m. on some idle Tuesday.
— Baz Luhrmann

Chapter Seven

The Night Before

Oakville, April 27, 2009

Bruce tried for months to help Daniel prepare his taxes for Cottage Concierge in order to meet the filing deadline at the end of April in 2009. He was frustrated by his son's inability to get his files organized; he wanted it done so that they could review the details together.

"Daniel, I am done with your taxes. You have no regard for my time."

Tension had been building for months between Daniel and his dad. Their bond was tested every day in personal arguments, especially about CC's taxes, so I took on the responsibility of being the go between. It had always been easy for Daniel and me to communicate. I thought that maybe I could take another approach and work with him to find ways to help him to think more clearly, so he could follow through on his commitments. And I did try, but nothing changed, no matter how much I gently pressed him about getting a day planner or focusing on commitments. My prompting was not at all helpful because even though his problems had appeared ordinary enough, he was not the Daniel we knew.

We began to notice once again that Daniel was disinterested, withdrawing from physical activities like golfing, playing basketball, or going to the gym. He had become more irritable again.

He was not in a position to concentrate on finishing his taxes for Cottage Concierge. He'd stare at the folders piled on his dad's desk, and make phone calls or get up and walk out of the room. He simply could not get the work done. It is difficult to see someone you love not being able to function normally. I carried on hoping things would improve. Meanwhile, Daniel's malaise escalated.

After dinner on Monday April 27, 2009, I cleaned up the kitchen and went into my office to return a few phone calls. While I was on the phone I heard Bruce and Daniel arguing in the kitchen.

"What is wrong with you, Daniel? Your taxes for Cottage Concierge have to be filed this week. Otherwise, you're going to pay heavy fines after the filing date."

"Dad, look, I've been at this all weekend. You've seen me. For two days I've been at it. I'm trying to get it done."

"What's stopping you from finishing the paperwork?"

"I can't find some of the receipts from my suppliers. And bank statements are missing from my files. I thought I had everything I needed to get the taxes done on time. I don't know. Maybe I left the receipts at the cottage last fall."

"Daniel, I'm tired of your excuses!"

"I'm trying to resolve this. I called my bank manger yesterday and she's going to make copies of the missing statements and fax them to me in the morning."

"But you still need to find those missing receipts. I

suggest you drive up north in the morning. Call your bank manager on the way to the cottage and tell her you'll be in Port Carling and you will pick up the statements in person."

"Okay. I'll drive up."

The arguing continued, Bruce and Daniel on opposite sides of the kitchen counter, a wall of anger rising up between them. Bruce had given his son the benefit of the doubt for too long. His patience had been worn down.

"Daniel, I have no problem helping you, I expected you to stay on top of your paperwork so that when the time came to file your taxes it wouldn't be a big deal. Now all I get is your excuses."

"Dad, when I'm at school I only have so much time to devote to CC."

After listening to the two of them, I walked out of my office and into the middle of their argument.

"Guys, please stop arguing. Nothing can be resolved tonight," I said.

I turned and looked directly at Daniel, purposefully speaking to him in a tone that wasn't accusatory. "Okay, Daniel, what can you do to get all of your paperwork in order by the end of the week? What can I do to help you?"

Daniel stared right through me. His face was blank. I knew it would take time for their bitter words to fade. But in that moment I felt for my son. I hoped they would find a way to work through their frustrations, their differences. I went back into my office off of the kitchen, and grabbed my book and quietly walked into the family room, out of their way, but still close enough.

Steaming from their argument, Bruce stormed out of

the kitchen and went into his office.

What is going on with our family? I thought. Wasn't it just last week that the five of us sat having dinner together, laughing and enjoying the delicious meal that Daniel had prepared for us? We also discussed plans for the summer, and Aimee finishing up her third year at university. We were having so much fun that I wished that the night would go on forever.

Daniel slammed his fist down on the counter and turned around to see me sitting on the sofa. His shoulders were slouched forward and I noticed that he had lost even more weight. His belt was cinched so tight around his waist that the excess leather strap fell down his pant leg. He had the look of desperation on his face. I felt helpless. There was nothing that I could do to bring peace into his life. I wanted to promise him that things would get better. Somehow.

Daniel walked away from the stacks of files that had lined our kitchen counters for days; he grabbed a Coors Light from the fridge and came over and sat near me in the family room. Sinking down into the soft cushions of the sofa, he stared down at the floor. His cloudy eyes reflected his malaise. His body language conveyed sadness, too. His head sank forward and he barely spoke. Daniel appeared physically exhausted in that moment. His usual fighting spirit was gone. I had the sense that my son was angrier with himself than anyone else.

"Daniel, you'll get this tax business behind you. Cottage Concierge has grown, and it might make sense now to have someone else manage the administrative side of the business."

"Mom, I have to deal with the 2008 taxes before I can

do anything else. I'll go up north tomorrow and get the statements and receipts."

"Do you want me to come with you?"

"You don't have to do that, Mom. I'll go up in the morning and be back before dinner."

"Daniel, don't let this get you down. We'll get through this. Maybe we can make a meal together tomorrow?"

"Sure, that'll be good."

At least talking about preparing a meal together made him smile. The argument between Bruce and Daniel had created a toxic atmosphere. I had taken Daniel's side as, I often did—right or wrong. But I felt that his father was too hard on him. I had watched angrily as the dialogue escalated from questions to accusations. I also knew that Daniel had become defensive in his dad's presence. Their relationship had become so complicated. In recent years Daniel's common refrain was, "He doesn't understand me, Mom."

And yet it was Bruce who was his best supporter when it came to launching Cottage Concierge.

That night, I gave up trying to be the bridge between my husband and my son.

Daniel and I were both drained and tired, so we trudged off to bed. Maybe a good night's sleep for everyone would help to soothe our nerves. And Daniel had a long drive ahead of him in the morning. As we walked up the back stairs together, I told him how much I loved him and that we would get past this difficult time. Soon we would be up north at the cottage.

"'Night, Ma. See you tomorrow," he said, and headed into his bedroom.

In my own room, I felt a strong urge to go back to

see Daniel again. I had to express to him how much his father and I loved him. I walked back down the hall toward his room. His door was partially open. He was in his bathroom. I called out to him.

"Daniel, I want you to know how much your dad and I love you. Can I have a hug?"

Daniel came out of the bathroom. He was holding a piece of dental floss in one hand and hugged me with the other.

"Sure, Mom."

"Why don't you take my truck tomorrow? The brakes on your truck are not great,

right?"

"Okay."

The offer of my truck seemed to linger in the air.

"Actually that would be good, thanks, Mom. Love you, see you in the morning." A stirring fragment of time. A conversation I will never forget.

The next morning we awoke to a crisp, late-spring day. The argument from the night before hung in the air, although Bruce and Daniel managed to talk with each other as if nothing was wrong. To their credit, they did not talk about taxes. Instead Bruce rhymed off the many jobs that needed to be done at home and at our cottage. We ate our breakfast thinking that this was just another ordinary day.

"Daniel, there's a lot of work for you here and at the cottage this summer. When you get back today, we can go over what has to be done."

Talking calmly to each other seemed to break through the heaviness between them. I was thankful for that. We exchanged keys for the trucks and made sure Daniel had his set of keys to the cottage.

"Is there gas in your truck, Lynn?" Bruce asked.

"I filled it yesterday."

As we walked to our vehicles, Daniel turned to Emily.

"Em, want me to take you to school?"

"Thanks, Daniel, that's nice of you."

Knowing that there would be a lot of traffic, Bruce discouraged Daniel's offer to drive his sister to school.

"You should head out now, Daniel. You might be able to miss rush-hour traffic."

"Yeah, okay. Hey, Em, take you another day."

"Sure, DK."

We were all leaving the house at the same time. I stood directly across from Daniel, who was getting ready to jump into my truck.

"Drive carefully," I called.

Walking over to the driver's side of the truck I hugged Daniel one more time and told him to text me when he got to the cottage. We went our separate ways.

Chapter Eight

The Moment

Oakville, June 21, 2010

There is a driving rain out my back door today. A downpour that reflects the heaviness in my heart. Inside this hard place I will try and go back to the moment when our lives changed forever.

During the morning of Tuesday, April 28, 2009, I had decided to forgo my marathon training for a mid-morning nap on the couch. I fell into a deep sleep and awoke to the sound of the phone ringing. The irregular ring tone made me think it was Daniel, calling from the cottage. I jumped up and ran to my office before the call went to voicemail.

"Hi, Daniel."

"Hi, Mom, how are you?"

"Good. I was having a nap before taking Bailey out for a walk."

"Oh. Sorry I woke you up."

"It's all right. It was time I got up."

"Have you had your meeting at the bank yet?" I asked.

"Not yet. It's at two this afternoon."

"How was the drive?"

"Not bad. Traffic was light. Mom, I've been thinking about the summer and my business. Once I get the taxes done for 2008, I can focus on the summer. I've spoken to some of my clients from last year and I've already booked some spring clean-up jobs for next month."

"Daniel, that's great news. I have some more names of people who may be interested in hiring you this summer. "

"It's going to be a great summer. I can feel it. I can't wait to be up here for good."

I didn't inquire any further. Daniel's tone suggested that he was upbeat and positive. It seemed to me that my son had gained a fresh perspective from his time alone on the drive.

Daniel had often spoken about the idea of Cottage Concierge as a year-round business. Our phone conversation that morning was like so many conversations that we'd had. Daniel appeared engaged in his work and his life. We do not always take the time to read between the words that are spoken. We look for the good.

Our conversation turned toward what I was doing.

"I was exhausted. I didn't feel like running this morning, but I'm planning to swim later today."

Daniel had always been interested in hearing about my training. So we discussed the idea of him coming to watch my next race.

Then I asked: "What did you have for lunch today?"

"Chicken. I made a sandwich this morning."

Food was always part of our conversations, especially since he had recently become an accomplished chef. In the past we talked about food because of his allergies, but it was on a different footing now. We talked about having sirloin burgers and a mixed green salad, so that Daniel and his dad could get to his taxes right after dinner. Ending our call, we agreed to talk again when he was back on the highway.

"I'll call you later, Mom."

"Great, DK, love you."

He responded the way he did at the end of every phone conversation, text and email: "Love you, Mom."

I hung up the phone and went on with my day.

After lunch, I got into Daniel's truck and drove to Burlington to join my swim group. Feeling rejuvenated after the intense swim practice, I was glad that I had pushed myself.

I was excited that Daniel was joining us for dinner. It signaled the beginning of summer and the return of our family living together under one roof.

No sooner did I climb back into my truck for the ride home than my cell phone rang. Digging into the contents of my swim bag, I finally found my phone. But I could see that I had missed several phone calls that afternoon, and they were all from Daniel. I punched in his cell phone number and waited. A few seconds later Daniel answered.

"Hi, Mom."

"I'm sorry. I missed your calls."

Something in his voice made me think he was tired.

"Do you feel okay to drive home?" I asked him.

"Yeah, I'm good. Finished my meeting at the bank and I am going back to the cottage to eat something before I head back."

Our conversation was unmemorable because it was so typical. Plans for dinner.

The approaching summer. During our call the cell service kept cutting out. So we agreed to talk later, on his drive home.

It was five o'clock and Emily and I were at home. My daughter was in her room doing homework and I was alone in the kitchen making dinner, slicing tomatoes and cucumbers, rinsing the lettuce and chopping peppers. I tossed all of the ingredients into my big white salad bowl. I defrosted ground sirloin so that I could make my homemade burgers.

After preparing our meal, I called Emily and we went off to watch my niece, Sierra, play a late-season hockey game at an arena close to home. I remembered that Daniel and I had agreed to talk on his way home.

"Emily, can you call Daniel?"

"What do you want me to tell him?"

"Ask him what time he thinks he'll be home so I can start the BBQ."

"Mom, his cell is going to voice mail. Should I text him?"

"Good idea, hon. Let him know what we're doing, and if he is near Oakville tell him to come by and watch Sierra's hockey game."

Daniel didn't see a lot of his younger cousin while he was away at school. But she thought he was amazing. Emily sent her brother a text. We hopped out of the truck. My parents were already there. We settled into our seats at the rink and watched my ten-year- old niece as she flew down the ice. At some point during the game, Sierra looked up and saw us in the stands. A big grin lit up her young face.

A few minutes to seven, I looked down at my watch.

Daniel would be home soon, I told myself. I signaled to Emily that we should leave. We said good-bye to my parents and took off toward home.

The moment that would change our lives was approaching.

Back home, we waited as the clocked ticked off the minutes and then hours. It was a school night and it was getting late, so I suggested that we eat.

"Let's eat, and I'll make a plate for Daniel; he can have it when he gets home."

Bruce sighed as he paced in and out of the kitchen; he was frustrated with Daniel's lack of communication. I felt worried, not frustrated. Why was it taking Daniel so long to get home? I started to think of possible reasons he was late, and what was stopping him from calling us. To put aside those unsettling thoughts I went about tidying up the kitchen and helping Emily with her homework.

In the kitchen I noticed Bruce's cell phone sitting on the edge of the countertop where it was being charged. The flashing red light indicated that a message was waiting. The red light made my heart beat faster. I walked over to read the new message. It was from Daniel. "Got away late. Going to Connor's house in Toronto to drop off an income tax form. Grabbing something to eat on my way."

I felt a sense of relief, although Bruce was not buying Daniel's excuse for being late.

Some time after eight p.m., maternal worry slipped back into my consciousness. I grabbed my cell phone and went into another room to try and reach Daniel. Within minutes I received a short response:

"Terrible traffic, love, DK."

That was the entire text. I showed the message to Bruce. Emily was also in the kitchen with us. She seemed frozen to the floor as she stood beside us. Bruce and I looked at each other in ways that only parents who are terrified do. Emily left us and ran up to her room where she sent her brother a text: "Daniel, mom and dad are really worried! Please get in touch with us!"

Daniel and I had spoken at four p.m. that day: "I'm packing my things now, Mom. I met with my bank manager this afternoon. Got everything I need from her. I might have a rest before heading home."

"Okay, dear. Call me when you're close to home. Love you, DK."

"Love you too, Mom. See you soon."

That evening, when we were wondering about when we should eat, we had no idea that Daniel was in the fight of his life. Chatting amiably, the three of us ate our hamburgers and then I made a plate for Daniel and put it in the fridge. After dinner, Bruce complained about Daniel's sudden change of plans.

"I wish Daniel could just be up front with us. You've gone to the trouble of making dinner and he decides at the last minute to do something else!"

At nine p.m. Daniel still had not returned home. Bruce sent another text message to him:

"DK, where are you? Let us know when you think you'll be home."

Messages like this went back and forth for about an hour. We'd send a text message and Daniel would respond with a few words:

"Sure Dad, just at Connor's."

After that text message, Bruce replied with more urgency.

"Daniel! What time will you be home?"

"Soon," he replied.

Daniel's responses were abrupt, but what was more troubling was how disconnected his responses were. Where was he? I thought he had told us he was on his way home several hours ago. Then, at the last minute he decided to see a friend in Toronto. But that would be so out of his way. Why was he going to find something to eat? I'd made dinner for him hours ago. Fear washed over me, making me feel lightheaded. I was beginning to panic. My throat tightened as I began to have strange thoughts. For some reason, a reason I didn't understand, we were not reaching our son. Something was happening that we couldn't grasp, and yet we both had a strange sense that things weren't right. Soon, both Bruce and I were frantically texting our son. It was so unlike Daniel to be this evasive, even cryptic, in his messages to us.

Then a text from Daniel to Bruce, sometime before ten p.m.: "Heading west, love DK."

And then nothing but a haunting silence.

The start of knowing something was wrong released an inexplicable dread and anxiety beyond anything that I had ever experienced. It became hard to focus. I was unsure what to do next. As my apprehension grew I began pacing the halls. I went upstairs to my bedroom to watch some television; I hoped some sitcom chatter would drown my fears. In this slowly expanding space of time, we were trapped inside a period of hours where we knew something was not right. Bruce and I could not be in the same room together. Our distress was too massive.

Aimee was at the University of Western Ontario, in London, studying for her final exam of the term. I didn't want to alarm her. Knowing that I couldn't hide my concern, I picked up the phone only to put it back down again. I would spare my daughter the worry.

Around ten forty-five p.m. there was still no word. I went back downstairs to let my dog out before bed. Bruce sat in silence in the family room. I walked over to him.

"Did you get any response from Daniel?"

"No, only the same one about 'heading home.' Nothing since then."

"Bruce, I'm scared. I can't sit still. I just feel something isn't right."

"Go to bed, hon, I'll let you know if I hear anything."

My husband's emotions had shifted from anger to fear; he took big, gulping breaths as if he was trying to suck fresh energy from someplace deep inside. Animalistic. I was close to incoherent. We were each moving toward an intense out-of-body experience, and it became difficult to talk to one another. It felt as though the act of confiding our terror would make our worst fears come true.

My husband was doing what he could to comfort me, but I would not be able to close my eyes, worrying about our son. I knelt down and gave him a hug, and went back to my room. This time to call Aimee. My daughter picked up the phone on the first ring.

"Hi, Mom."

"Hi, Aimee, how's the studying going tonight?"

"Not bad, Mom. I'll be so glad when the exam is over tomorrow."

"You must be exhausted, love."

"Yeah, I am, Mom."

"Dear, have you spoken to Daniel this evening?"

"No. I haven't talked to him since last week. Not since last Thursday night, when he insisted that I go for a drive with him to get the brakes fixed on his truck.

"Oh, right," I said.

"Remember, he pleaded with me to go with him, to keep him company. He was silly . . . so funny that day. Why, what's up?"

"I'm not sure, but Daniel went up north earlier today in my truck. He said that he'd be home for dinner. And then he texted us to say that he was going to see Connor in Toronto before coming home."

Aimee recalled conversations with friends that day.

"I think Daniel and Marissa texted today. I'll get in touch with her. What about Ryan? Have you contacted him?"

"No, dear. We've been trying to reach Daniel."

"Mom, I know Ryan has a new Blackberry and I think I have his PIN. I'll call you back."

We said good-bye and hung up.

I continued wandering in and out of rooms on the second floor of our home. I considered going into Emily's room to talk, but she was asleep. I closed her door and went back to my room.

Then I heard the double ring of a long distance call; I immediately thought it was Daniel. I was sure that he was calling to apologize for being late, and that he'd be home soon. We could breathe again. Bruce picked up the phone in the kitchen. I could hear him talking so I picked up the phone in our bedroom. Aimee was calling from London. Bruce hung up.

"Mom, I was telling Dad that no one has heard from Daniel tonight. Ryan has been trying to reach him all day, but Daniel has not returned any of his messages."

"This is so unlike your brother. His phone is usually always on him."

"Marissa just responded to my text. I'll read it to you," Aimee continued. "She says that they exchanged texts today. Daniel told her he was doing well, and he was going up north for files or something like that. She told him to have a nice time, and that was the end of their text conversation."

"Sounds like a normal conversation between them, but I can't help feel that something is happening to us. I'm scared."

"Why, Mom?"

"Last night, Daniel and your Dad got into an argument about CC's taxes. All of Daniel's paperwork was neatly stacked on the counters in the kitchen. I could tell he was doing his best to be organized. But they both were tired and lost patience with each other."

"Mom, remind me why Daniel was going to the cottage?" Aimee asked.

"Daniel was going to look for receipts at the cottage, and then see his bank manager to collect statements from last year."

Aimee told me about the day when she and I returned home from spending a few days at the cottage earlier in the month.

"Do you remember when we came home from the

cottage last week and Daniel was standing in the kitchen with all of his files, Daniel told me that day that he couldn't get it done. He said, "All I have done this afternoon is walk around the kitchen looking at these files. I just can't do it anymore."

Looking back now, I can see that Daniel's life was slowly being destroyed. Sleeplessness, isolation, and weight loss were part of it. The Daniel we knew was falling fast, his life imploding. He wasn't in a position to see where his problems might end. The massive effort it took for Daniel to conceal his emotional state must have been overwhelming for him.

Chapter Nine

DK Goes North

Sometimes I try to imagine the last hours of Daniel's life. I try in the hope I will come to understand why our son ended his life. I replay the scenario over and over, but it never brings the comfort I'm looking for.

Oakville April 28, 2009.
Daniel had turned his cell phone off and tuned the world out. Chances are Daniel walked through the cottage trying to figure out what to do about his painful emotional state.

Daniel went to the bathroom off of the narrow hallway and brushed his teeth. His toothpaste and spit sat in the sink for months. It was our last living particle of him and we were unable to wash it away. Daniel opened the doors to the front hall closet and took down my old winter jacket. The night was getting colder. He put it on and walked outside. Maybe he went out toward the water so he could remember what the bay looked like in late spring. Daniel was letting go.

As the late April day grew darker, Daniel's ideation continued to build. Continuous thoughts about death and the method in which to end life would have now consumed him. There would have been no one around to intervene. After Daniel turned off his phone he moved farther into darkness; despair had overwhelmed him.

That fateful spring day had begun with sunny skies and warm temperatures. Then the weather changed. The skies grew dark, and Daniel would have been bathed in twilight shadows while he sat alone on the couch. The television was the only source of light in the room.

Then Daniel got up and walked into the kitchen, where our family photographs are scattered on the top of the bar counter. Daniel may have noticed the reflection of himself in the stainless steel fridge.

Then, slowly, Daniel began to feel some relief. For the first time that evening his mind was not muddled. On that spring night he realized that he had separated himself from his family. The momentary control of his feelings felt good. He moved quickly through the cottage, with his plan hovering at the edge of his thoughts. While he had been in the kitchen he had opened the small bar fridge, pulled out a beer, and thought about writing his final communication to his family members who were trying desperately to reach him.

He grabbed one of the lined notepads and the black pen that he kept in his desk drawer in the small reading room, and wrote his last words:

Dear Mom, Dad, Emily and Aimee, I am sorry for lying, and trying to hide things from you. I covered up my problems. I know I've disappointed you. I am sorry.

Daniel was left-handed and wrote with his entire hand

moving all over the page. His final dispatch spoke of intense hopelessness:

I drank to escape, but drinking wasn't doing anything for me anymore. Don't blame yourselves cause you did everything for me.
Love, Forever & Always DK

The elixir, which once alleviated Daniel's anxiety and hushed his depressive thoughts, was no longer useful. With his last words he unburdened himself of trying to live the lives of two Daniels.

As Daniel placed the note down on the counter he noticed our faces beaming from photographs of another happier summer. His note and our memories would be all that remained. Then Daniel walked out the front door of our cottage.

He shut the door behind himself, and the wreath that announced JOY would have banged hard against the glass pane. Daniel jumped up onto one of the stone columns on the front porch, his final thoughts disappearing into the night sky.

On the evening of Tuesday April 28, 2009, we lost all contact with our son.

I lie awake and conjure up images of Daniel outside, as he stepped up onto that stone column. Was he thinking that he could stop himself? Did he mean to take himself close to edge of life, but not to suicide?

When it came to snowboarding or wakeboarding, he would push himself to the edge. As a teenager, Daniel took every opportunity to leap off boathouses and rock cliffs. Many of the other kids at the cottage did the same things, jumping off high diving boards and moving at high speed through the water. I never thought that this behaviour could be an indicator of major depression. And I still don't believe it is. The hard truth is that we had no understanding of depression and disorders of the brain, and the potential for a catastrophic outcome.

. . . .

The next morning Bruce took Emily to school and then he planned to drive north to find our son. After they left the house, I took my dog, Bailey, and drove to a park overlooking Lake Ontario. I was trying to escape reality. I was completely stricken.

Bruce received the news of Daniel's suicide first and then immediately called my cell phone. I couldn't run away any longer. In that moment I knew that I would be forced to face a life without Daniel. I answered my phone.

"Lynn, where are you?"

"I don't want to know anything!"

"Hon, tell me where you are. I'll come and get you."

"No, I don't want you to find me. I know something has happened to Daniel. I don't want to know anything right now."

"Lynn, the news is not good. We need to be together. We have to get the girls."

"Oh my God, Bruce."

"I promise I'll take care of you. You have to tell me where you are."

. . . .

The previous night Bruce had called John Newton and asked him to see if lights were on at our cottage. John told Bruce that it was dark over at our place and said he would go over to our cottage in the morning.

"I'll check things out," he promised.

True to his word, John wandered over to our cottage in the early morning hours. Walking up our drive-way he came upon the terrifying death scene. As John stood there absorbing the shocking image, perhaps he thought about the young man he had watched grow from a little boy to an adult. Maybe he remembered all the happy times our families had spent together—the golf matches with his son, Peter, and Bruce and Daniel, affectionately referred to as "the dads and lads". He may have recalled the philosophical conversations he had had with our son, or reflected on the day that he spoke to Daniel and cautioned him about his drinking.

They shared a memorable history.

Two months went by before I could meet face to face with John. He had witnessed the scene of our son's death, and I was immersed in grief. Because of the circumstances surrounding the death of our son, paramedics and police both arrived around nine a.m. The paramedics found no vital signs in Daniel; however, they still initiated resuscitation. But death had occurred hours before, and nothing could be done.

John immediately called our home in Oakville. He had to leave a message, as everyone was out of the house.

"Keanes, it's John. Get in touch with me right away."

John may have made a reference to a problem, but I don't recall. I do know that when I listened to his message sometime later in the day, I shook uncontrollably listening to the regret in his voice.

John Newton walked through the cottage after the paramedics and police had left.

He collected Daniel's clothes and placed them on the top mattress of his bunk bed. He opened the front door of the cottage and walked down the winding road, wondering how he would tell his good friends about the death of their son.

Daniel was officially pronounced dead at our cottage on the morning of Wednesday, April 29, 2009. *Cause of death: Asphyxiation.*

The night before, when Bruce first told the police that we couldn't get in touch with our son, they asked us for a photograph of Daniel. They told him that this was routine police procedure when a family member is missing. The photograph that we sent was of Daniel sitting on the fireplace at the cottage in his board shorts (the same shorts he went north in) and a brown-and-blue-striped polo shirt. It is a typical Daniel shot. Tilted head, hands clasped on his knees, wondering why his mom insists on taking so many pictures.

Chapter Ten

Aftermath

Oakville April 29, 2009

On the afternoon of the worst day of our lives Bruce and I drove to Emily's high school. Having to tell our youngest child that her brother had died was so unfair. So out of the order of life. Our kids were supposed to grow old together. There was no easy way to deliver bad news.

Bruce got out of the truck, slamming the door. He disappeared into the school's foyer, and within a few minutes both of them appeared on the steps at the front of the school. I got out of the truck and walked towards them. Emily was shaking and her face was red from crying. She looked helplessly at me. I was her mom but I couldn't make this better for her.

"Mom, did Daniel die? What's going on?"

I nodded because I couldn't speak.

Emily asked again: "Is that why we didn't hear from him last night?"

She began sobbing.

"Oh, Daniel."

Emily slid into the back seat of the truck and dropped her head into her hands.

As we drove toward London to pick up Aimee, our crying sounded like soft chants. As parents there was nothing we could do to change our circumstances. We were now a family of four, not five.

As Bruce drove, I climbed over the console into the backseat so that I could hold her in my arms. There I was, sitting in the back of the truck, massaging Emily's small, trembling hands as we drove west along the highways. During our drive Aimee tried calling us several times. She knew that we had not been able to reach her brother, and she was worried. Because we didn't answer, Aimee began to fear the worst.

Each time one of our cell phones buzzed, I said, "Please don't answer the call."

However Emily felt differently.

"Aimee and I texted this morning. She is so upset. If we don't answer her it will make things worse. We should answer her. Don't you think?"

"Emily, I understand, but we don't know if Aimee is alone or if someone is with her. We'll be there soon. I know she's waiting to hear from us, dear, but we have to tell her about Daniel in person."

When we finally arrived at Aimee's apartment there were U-Haul moving vans everywhere. Parents were running in and out of the apartment building trying to get their kids packed up for summer. Aimee was upstairs in her unit, so Bruce and Emily took the one open elevator to her floor. When they got off the elevator they walked down the hall toward her apartment door, which was propped open with packed boxes and garbage bins. When Aimee saw her sister's and her dad's desperate expressions, she understood.

Immediately, Bruce reached his arms out and cradled his now-eldest child.

"Aimee, I'm so sorry hon, but it's not good."

"What?" Aimee replied. "Dad, what happened?"

"The police said that sometime last night Daniel took his life at the cottage."

"Dad, no! Please no!"

Slowly, Aimee understood that Daniel had slipped away from us in the night. We had gone from being an ordinary family to survivors of suicide.

We drove back to our home in silence. There were no words for the unimaginable feelings we had in those few hours driving home to Oakville.

As we turned onto our street, I dreaded the thought of walking into our house. Our home, the home that held so many wonderful family memories, now contained death.

A police cruiser sat in front of our house with two officers, whose job description included notifying parents of their child's suicide. Earlier that day I had received the first news about Daniel from my husband. I wasn't going to hear it again from the police. As they walked toward us I ran to the side door, opened it, and then shut it quickly behind me. My brother was standing inside in the hallway, by the door. He held me in his arms until I stopped trembling.

"What am I going to do without Daniel?" I buried my face into his chest as I wept.

"Lynn, whatever you need. I'll be here for you and your family. I promise."

The real world's response to a suicide is to try and be supportive of those who are dealing firsthand with loss; however, the real world goes on in spite of your tragedy.

Meanwhile, we, the newly bereaved, remain stuck in the moment that our world changed. And we aren't always able to reach out for help because what we need, we can't have.

We had only been home a few minutes, but I needed to go back outside. This time I walked out to the backyard and sat on one of the stone steps. The garden was coming alive in the heat of the late spring. The grass below my feet felt cool as I rocked side to side, holding the pain in my arms. I needed the fresh air; hoped it would clear my head. I remember feeling like our family was literally dissolving. How do I live in this world without my child? The warmth of the late afternoon sun beat down on my neck.

I sat down in that particular spot for a reason. A few years back, when I had been working on the garden in our yard, I'd been out shopping and had come across a small bronze statue of *The Thinker* by Rodin and bought it. Daniel helped me out by placing the statue among a patch of wildly pink hydrangeas. And on that first day of death I felt that Daniel was guiding me to come and sit, away from the business going on in our home as news spread about his death.

"Daniel, why did you die?" I screamed. "I miss you!"

And on and on, I sat by myself, raging and yearning for my son. I knew that our son had died, but in that space of time between hearing of his death and picking up our remaining children I had asked my husband not to tell me anything more. I was trying to process our tragedy. After several minutes, Aimee came outside, looking for me. When she found me, she sat down beside me and gently placed her arm around my shoulder.

We sat there together for a long time, staring into the flowering gardens.

In the quiet of the moment, she said, "Mom, I know you will make something good come from this."

In the tumble of emotions that hit me, I understood for the first time that Daniel had taken his life. My first thought was that he must have been in tremendous pain.

Surprisingly, I did not feel the shame attached to suicide. We stood up, holding onto each other, and walked back into our house.

During the rest of the day I sat in the family room, on the sofa, near the black and white photograph of my son, hoping that if I stared hard into his eyes, our nightmare would mysteriously end, and he would walk through the door as he always did. The night before I had been riddled with panic, and uncertain of our son's whereabouts, but I held onto a belief that he was all right. He would come home. Then Bruce and I would sit down with him and figure out what was bringing him down. We would try to understand his problems, calmly. I realize now that those thoughts may have kept me from getting in the truck and heading north to save our son.

Oakville, May 1, 2009

A few days later, we sat in our kitchen, staring out the window, asking ourselves, "Why—why did this happen to our son?

I will never understand why Daniel ended his life," Bruce said.

"I don't think we'll ever truly understand hon," I replied.

Bruce and I ambled around our home hoping for any

sign of Daniel, even a trace of his musky scent. Something—anything that we could attach ourselves to in order to feel his presence. Staring out at a world that was still in progress while ours had stopped.

Nothing mattered.

One night, after I'd gone to bed, Bruce came into our room to talk as I lay with the covers pulled up around my neck.

"Why didn't he come to you, Lynn? You two were so connected, and I know how much you love him."

"I knew Daniel had his struggles, but never to this degree," I replied.

After our son's death, Bruce contacted Daniel's school. The registrar's office told him that Daniel Keane was not enrolled in classes. The marks he had provided on a spreadsheet that spring were false.

Each week after his death it seemed as though we were uncovering another part of our son's life. Daniel's friends told us that Daniel had been a great friend and the life of the party. They also said that he would go underground and not communicate with them for days. His manic and depressive states dictated his behaviour.

In his note he told us he was sorry. I wonder if he was sorry for what was about to take place in our lives? He could not see the son, brother, and friend that we all cherished.

Chapter Eleven

Wasteland

Oakville, May 2, 2009

I loved being in the middle of Daniel's world. I was en-amoured of his charisma, and that made it harder for me to see that he had not been functioning normally. When we were together, he behaved as if things were okay. Life was good. And I allowed myself to be lulled into thinking that our family bond would sustain us. In the days after his death, I awoke to unimaginable heartbreak. The common thread of sadness that greets mourners each day is remarkably banal. We are stirred awake by something that almost feels normal, and then, in a matter of seconds, gives way to a complete bodily ache. Now I understood the mournful wail of the loon whose baby had slipped away under a cloudless night.

In those first days, my bed was a wasteland of sorrow. I didn't want to linger under the covers, but I didn't want to get up and be part of another day, either. The days after loss are torture. There is no reprieve. I learned to adapt to the gravity of grieving. I brushed my teeth in grief and got dressed in grief. I saw friends and made lists so I didn't forget, because grief keeps one from remembering what one needs to do. My eyelids felt heavy from sleepless nights and crying.

As I sat up in bed I noticed that someone had parted the drapes to reveal a spectacular blue sky. But the brutal facts hit me again, and I fell back into bed and screamed into my pillow. In the kitchen, there were days' worth of dirty teacups and glasses. Our bed was littered with magazines and books. Everything was left where it was last used. Disorder was my newfound companion.

Dust particles were collecting on the surface of the dark walnut furniture in our room. The shape of my body had been imprinted on the bed sheets. I was losing weight, spending most of my time lying in bed. Embellished cushions and duvets sat at the foot of the bed in a heap. I began living in a messy world the day that Daniel died.

I was so completely disconnected with the present that I was not able to grasp the details surrounding his death. After John found Daniel, how long before the ambulance arrived? Who took Daniel from the cottage to Bracebridge? Where was he now? Who would be bringing him to Oakville? I felt like an animal caught in a wicked trap. I was alive but slowly dying as I lay in the twisted folds of my blankets.

As I lay languishing, I began writing Daniel's notice. I could not say the word "obituary" yet. That would make the events of the past few days so final. Parents are not supposed to write their children's obituaries or plan for their burials.

Awake and alone in my bedroom, some divine respite washed over me and I managed to write his obituary:

Suddenly, on Tuesday, April 28, 2009, our beloved

Daniel was taken from us to be with God. The joy that he brought to each of us has been silenced. Everyone he met throughout his life was warmed by his laughter and his enthusiasm for life . . . . Daniel Keane, of Oakville, Ontario, will always be Lynn and Patrick's (Bruce) cherished son, devoted brother to Aimee and Emily, and a beloved grandson and nephew. His warm smile and his humour will continue to guide us in each new day.

When I began writing Daniel's obit, I noticed that I felt oddly better. Thinking about him in such an intimate and self-possessed manner allowed me to feel his presence.

Words charged with emotion came tumbling onto the page before I could even grasp what I was thinking. Twenty-three wonderful years together reduced to a short column in the newspaper.

Chapter Twelve

Elegy

Oakville, May 5, 2009

The night before Daniel's funeral we went to view his body. Even in my emotional mess I knew that this was important. The purpose, I'm told, is to have closure. I still don't understand the concept. My family searched for many things after Daniel's death, but we have never looked for closure.

As I stood in front of our son I could still hear my husband's voice in my head: "It's not good."

I stood gazing at Daniel's smooth skin and dark brown hair. His long fingers looked puffy now, but allowing myself to see him in this state was what I needed to do. He looked tall as he lay there. I had the sensation that his spirit had left the physical body the day he died, but the boy and the man that grew up and taught us many life lessons was in front of us.

Oakville, May 6, 2009

On the morning of Daniel's funeral I wandered into my dressing room where I keep several photographs of our kids. The photograph of Daniel and I at our cottage at Christmas instantly caught my attention. The shot was taken in front of the glass doors that overlooked a snow-covered bay. Daniel is sitting on a counter barstool and I am leaning into him with my arm around his shoulder. In the photograph I can see our easy, mother-son bond. I lifted the picture to my lips and gently kissed his image. I whispered, "I love you, Daniel."

Beside the photographs lay a book that I had given Daniel as a gift in high school, when he was immersed in rap culture. I had found the book the night before in his room, and a piece of lined paper had fallen to the ground. As I unfolded the paper I realized that it was Daniel's 2009 list for school and his summer business, Cottage Concierge. He had written the list the week before after his dad insisted that he "get organized" for the summer.

The contents of his list were:

- CC 2008 Financials
- HR Management Assignment Class notes
- Transcripts
- Budget to progress from present to May 1st and from May 1st to Sept 1st.

Some of the lines had been highlighted in yellow marker by Daniel, suggesting that the work still needed his attention. Other lines had a small checkmark: job completed.

There were so many unanswered questions. Daniel was not at school in the spring of 2009. Why did he have an entry about class notes on his list? He was obviously looking ahead, planning his 2009 summer business budget. I truly felt that Daniel was trying to make it to the summer. I think the fact that it fell out of this book on the eve of his funeral was serendipitous; that and the fact that I was the one to find the list and know that he was trying. I put the note back between the pages of the book. The right-hand corner of the first page of *The Rose That Grew From Concrete* was folded over where I had written a short note to Daniel on his seventeenth birthday in reference to the late rapper, Tupac Shakur:

March 3, 2004
Dear Daniel, I know he is gone. But perhaps, Tupac's words are his legacy to all who follow him.
   Love Mom & Dad

That night I sat on the floor of Daniel's bedroom reading each page of the book. Even in my sleep-deprived state I knew that this was what I had been searching for. I had found a way through his sparse, elegant verse to participate in my son's funeral.

When the plans were being made for the service, I had purposely distanced myself. I was not going to be an accomplice at my son's funeral. For the first time since we received the news of Daniel's sudden death, I was able to function. I would recite Tupac's elegiac poem, *If There Be Pain.*

Standing in front of my bathroom mirror, I felt calm. I looked like hell. But the image in the mirror reminded me of my old self, and applying makeup that morning felt like such a simple act on an extraordinary day.

"Mom, you look good for fifty-one," Daniel would say.

I imagined his throaty voice in my head. On so many

occasions, Daniel would come into my bathroom and stand directly in front of the mirror just as I was doing. He usually wanted my opinion on something to do with his hair or clothes. And then he'd make me laugh with one of his many dialects before I rushed him out of my bathroom so I could get ready.

Walking out of the bathroom, I stopped in my dressing room once again, this time to put on the strand of pearls that my husband had given to me many years ago. Black dress and pearls—a classic pairing.

Before I left the room, I picked up Tupac Shakur's book. Later that day I would find some inner strength to read the words of the late rap artist.

I closed the book and turned off the lights. As I walked down the hall toward my daughters' bedrooms, I heard muffled laughter and the whir of a blow dryer coming from their shared bathroom. Walking into their private world, I felt a sense of lightness. Their brightly painted bathroom was where the two of them shared sisterly secrets. But on this very difficult morning they pulled me into their moment and I, too, was taken with how we could be so normal on such a cruel day.

"Mom, the pearls and dress are appropriate for today," Aimee said.

I helped Aimee with her zipper, and then Aimee straightened Emily's long, blonde, curly hair. When we had finished getting ready, I took both of the girls into my arms and held them tightly.

"I want you girls to know how much we love you."

In the depths of our sorrow we were still a family. We hugged, and soon began to cry. The heaviness of the day was sinking in. Leaving the girls' bathroom, we walked down to the kitchen where my husband was waiting for us. Bruce was standing by the kitchen counter, wearing a dark blue suit. He had lost weight and looked very tired. We had both aged several years over the past week. He was looking at his cell phone.

"Lynn, so many people are reaching out to us. I'll save the messages. Daniel touched a lot of people."

Initially, I read the sympathy cards and messages that filtered through our front door, or email, but it didn't take long for me to realize that these sentiments only underscored my pain. I stopped reading anything that wasn't in a book.

The morning of the funeral, I had purposely stayed upstairs, away from my husband. We reminded each other of our history as parents and the loss of our son. We were each other's worst trigger. In the first days, my grief was too profound to share, even with Bruce.

In the kitchen Bruce and I held onto one another, while Aimee and Emily looked at us. I motioned for them to come and join us.

We held each other and cried. And then we said a prayer for Daniel.

It used to be five of us launching forward in life, heading to the next adventure.

Now the four of us were fragile.

In those few hours on the morning of Daniel's funeral we were living as close to a normal day as we could. We had arranged to bring our son home from Bracebridge, where his body had been taken and where a toxicology test had been done. We had answered the door as people dropped in throughout the day and into the evening to offer their condolences. We had organized a service and burial. Mercifully, Bruce and Aimee took the lead and allowed me to remain in a fetal position in my bed during those first days.

Before we left our house, I lowered the blind on the side door. When we returned home we would appreciate our privacy. Shutting the door behind us we had no understanding of what was to follow.

As we walked the few steps to Bruce's truck, I felt the sting of an extraordinarily beautiful late spring morning. The problem was, we were not in any position to enjoy a day like this without Daniel. I reached into my purse for my sunglasses, which had become a protective shield, saving me from the curious.

. . . .

After the funeral luncheon, we said goodbye to our family and friends and drove home to our new life without Daniel.

Opening the door to our home, I thought I would die from the heaviness of my burden. Daniel was not coming home. I walked up the back steps that lead to his bedroom and collapsed on the top step. Crying out his name. Staring out at the world that looked very different to us. The protective cover of shock was lifting, and in its place was the worst physical and emotional pain I have ever experienced.

Chapter Thirteen

DK's Night in Toronto

Toronto, February 25, 2011
Bruce and I drove up and down College Street in silence trying to find Grace's Upstairs, a bistro in Toronto's west end. We didn't talk for most of the drive into the city from Oakville; a feeling of quiet desolation had settled on us since our son had died.

But Aimee had felt that it was time to honour her brother's life. She had been thinking about a celebration for a few months, and announced her plans one January night when the three of us were out for dinner. Immediately after Daniel's suicide, the four of us had talked about organizing a memorial celebration; however, after the funeral we put the idea out of our minds. We were unable to leave our home. We certainly weren't in a position to celebrate Daniel's life. But Aimee was insistent.

"I need to do this for Daniel," she told us. "It would have been his twenty-fifth birthday this March."

"How can we help?" I replied.

Bruce lowered his eyes without saying anything. I sensed that he wasn't sure if he was ready to handle this.

I understood. I also knew that the time when we could get Daniel's friends together was quickly passing.

Aimee added: "For now I wanted to see how you guys felt about the idea. I have to make some calls. But I want to have Daniel's night in Toronto. I hope you and mom are okay with that?"

From that point on, the memorial would be affectionately referred to as Daniel's Night in Toronto; a nod to his beloved band, The Tragically Hip, and their iconic song, "Bobcaygeon." Aimee had decided on the celebration for her brother, and the fact that her mom and dad couldn't get it together in public was not going to stop her.

That night would be the first real opportunity for Daniel's friends to come together in his memory.

On a blustery cold evening in late February in 2011, Bruce and I searched for the club where Aimee was hosting the celebration. Staring out of the frosted windows of the truck, my emotional resolve broke down. I realized that I wasn't ready to see Daniel's friends after all. What would his friends say to me? Their physical presence would only remind me that he was gone. I wanted to go home. Nothing these young people could do or say could possibly pull me out of my grief.

I felt Bruce's unease too. When he is stressed his sighs are heavy, full of the weight of his emotions. In our truck that night I listened to his long painful exhales, while staring out at the glittering snow dancing in a pool of moonlight.

I reminded myself that Aimee had put her heart into this night in honour of her brother. It was to come together and remember Daniel.

Bruce looked out of his window to see if he could find

the bar. "Is it Grace's? I think I see it across the street."

"That's it."

"Okay, good, I'll have to turn around to park."

We had made it to Grace's. First hurdle completed.

After we had found the bar, Bruce turned the truck around and headed towards the municipal parking lot. I was relieved that the lot was close to the venue, but I felt nervous and breathless. Our life without Daniel was poisoned by a new fear of the unexpected.

Everything we did felt awkward.

As my husband manoeuvered the truck into a packed downtown parking lot, I searched for coins for the parking meter. Sticking my fingers into the console I retrieved some loose change that immediately slipped out of my fingers and fell down between the console and the front seat. Then I looked for money in my purse, feeling our anxiety building.

As we left the truck and walked towards Grace's Upstairs, I looked at Bruce for reassurance.

"Hon, everything will be okay. I'll be beside you."

As Bruce was speaking to me, I realized that I had forgotten the journal that I had purchased so Daniel's friends could write down their recollections about him. It would be another portal into our son's life.

Bruce waited while I went back to retrieve the book. Walking toward the building, the significance of the night settled on my shoulders.

As we moved slowly up the narrow landing to Grace's Upstairs, conversations and Daniel's music came flooding down the staircase from the room above. Their happy revelry surprised me. At the top of the stairs I sucked up my pain just enough to enter the room; it was loaded with reminders of Daniel.

As we walked past the last step and into the middle of the lounge, our presence caused a hush in the room. The conversations seemed to stop as guests realized that Daniel's parents were in the room. One by one each person smiled or nodded in our direction, looking for a sign, something that would help them gauge our state. It had been twenty long months since Daniel had died.

Bob Marley's "Redemption Song" was playing loudly as we entered the room. I turned to walk towards Daniel's high school friends, and noticed that Bruce was already moving toward them. I watched as Daniel's teammates landed high fives on Bruce's palm and pulled him in towards their hearts. The exact hug that Daniel always gave his family. Now it was my turn to say hello.

Candles scattered all over the bar gave the room a warm and inviting glow that made me want to linger in the soft light forever.

For the evening, Aimee had put together a CD of all of her brother's music. The music reminded everyone of Daniel. Tunes from Bob Marley, The Tragically Hip, Dave Matthews, Neil Young, Led Zeppelin, Red Hot Chili Peppers, Pearl Jam, and so many others. The music was comfort for our aching souls.

One after another, Daniel's friends began approaching both Bruce and me, often just with an embrace, a hushed condolence, or to share an amusing story. Friends also came from Daniel's university and college days, including some of the guys who worked for Cottage Concierge. Some of them were friends of both Daniel and Aimee.

The massive mahogany bar was the focal point of the

room. At one end of the bar, near the tall windows that overlooked College Street, a group of young men had congregated. One of the young men, Ted, was sitting on a bar stool, intently writing in the journal that I had brought that evening.

Ted wrote:

Whatever Dan did he did it until it was done. Even if it meant long boarding into four lanes of oncoming traffic on St. Patrick's Day. He would not quit until he had his fill. Even when he got back to our house, face bloodied after falling hard. I can still picture that shit-eating grin on his face.

I walked up to him at the bar and introduced myself.

"Hi, I'm Dan's mom, Lynn."

"Nice to meet you. I'm Ted. I have a lot of stuff to write down. Dan and I spent a lot of time together."

I walked away, but Ted continued writing:

He was a selfless guy in my opinion, regardless of what was going on, even if he didn't have a dime to his name he would show up with what he had and give it to everybody.

The next few lines he wrote make me cry every time I read them:

His priorities were his friends, he gave and did not ask, he took and repaid in double and there was not a moment where I couldn't count on him. He was the man, hard as fuck but extremely fair and I am a lesser person because he is gone.

I made a point of finding Connor, the young man who had worked for Cottage Concierge during the summer of 2008. I wanted to see how he was doing; I knew that he had struggled with the death of his close friend.

"Lynn, Dan was like my teacher, that's how I think about him. He taught me how to paint, and cut down trees," Connor said.

"I know that Daniel appreciated how hard you worked that summer," I replied.

"For me it was a great job. I got to be with my buddy, and working outdoors, and wakeboarding all summer. It was sweet. Just great times."

"2008 was a great summer for Daniel, too," I said.

"He liked to have a good time and wanted to make sure everyone around him was having a good time, too. There was no one like Dan."

Connor and I hugged and promised to stay in touch. I haven't seen him since but what he said to me that night was all I needed to know.

Another friend greeted me.

"Hi, I'm Kyle Latour. Dan and I and a few other guys shared a house together in Waterloo."

"Yes, I remember we met then. Good to see you again," I said.

"I loved Dan. It is really hard without him to talk to. He and I spent so much time just talking about life. What we were going to do after school. I wanted to be a chef and so did he. But Dan wanted to open up a restaurant where anyone could eat. Especially people with food allergies. And we partied together, too. We used to call ourselves Partners in Crime. When Dan died, I got a tattoo on my chest in honour of our friendship."

He asked me if I would like to see it. I said yes. Kyle unbuttoned his plaid shirt to reveal a tattoo that was the size of a man's fist. It was a crest with the letters P.I.C. and Friends Forever in the centre. Then I began to feel sad. Kyle's pain was triggering my own.

My husband and I continued moving around the lounge, speaking with Daniel's good friends. Their honesty and openness was comforting.

Another friend, Mark, wrote about how he learned of his friend's suicide:

The night Dan went missing I was with Ryan Kemper. He (Ryan) called me in a panic. "Have you seen or talked to Dan?" I replied. "No". We sat up together till the morning to discover the worst. Dan never did anything solely for himself. His intentions were for the common good. Dan lived this every minute of his life. Success depends on those around. Dan taught me that.

Daniel's friends depended on him more than I realized. Just as his own family had done. It's funny but I never referred to my son as Dan; however, he was most surely their good friend, Dan, and I was thankful that each of them came to share their stories and remember a good life.

The next morning, all the memories and conversations about Daniel were stuck in my mind when I woke up, so I stayed in bed. Thinking about Daniel's Night in Toronto, I could only concentrate on my own sorrow. So I began to think about Daniel as a way to distract myself: what he looked like, how he walked on a slight angle in his flips flops and baggy pants and vintage T-shirts. He wore vintage because he threw all of his clothes into one or two loads, and in the process he washed the colour out of his clothes and faded others. But that was my Daniel, relaxed and easy. Somehow these good thoughts will soothe me so I can function. And that is how I get on. Two steps forward, ten steps back.

Chapter Fourteen

Alchemy of a Family

Estero, Florida, March 10, 2012

On a sun-soaked morning in Southwestern Florida I was getting set to participate in a 5-k charity race with a friend of Emily's who had joined us for March break. With less than fifteen minutes to the start the announcer introduced the American national anthem and after the stirring rendition, sung by a thirteen-year-old girl, the announcer called on the participants to chant, "we are the cure...we are the cure."

"C'mon everyone. Say it loud and proud. Because of you we will find a cure.

Say it. WE ARE THE CURE!"

The chant spread through the crowd of spectators and runners; the deafening sounds made me feel light-headed. Even though we were strangers, we were united in that moment.

Then she said: "We are here this morning. Some of us are survivors, family, and friends—but some are missing today."

I choked up, because all I could think about was Daniel. Yes, I was missing him this morning and every morning. Standing in the middle of the crowd of runners I experienced an unexpected well of grief. Tears ran down my face.

Oddly, I am thankful for those reckoning moments when grief won't let me forget the heartbreak, but it is also a reminder of my love for my son. I have to catch my breath but the memories are something to hold onto.

The starter's gun brings me back. Drinking in the sunshine I wipe away the tears and look down at my *Daniel 23* tattoo. And I think to myself that today, I will run for you, Daniel.

Bonita Beach (Post Race)
The luxury of falling asleep on the beach is something that I will never tire of doing. Unfortunately, the two women sitting near me were intent on talking as loudly as they could, wiping out the natural beach noises that I was relying on to induce sleep.

"Look at those girls walking down by the water. Not an ounce of fat on them," Woman 1 said.

"Yeah. I used to have a figure like that. But I never appreciated it when I was younger. I took it for granted," Woman 2 said.

Most of us are not that different from the women I sat next to on the beach. We don't always appreciate what we have.

As the afternoon progressed, I moved my lounge chair closer to the edge of the gulf. I watched the grey pelicans' massive beaks smacking the surface of the water in search of food. The late-day tides were bringing in a fresh harvest of fish for the birds.

A little blonde boy and his mother came into my view.

The boy had a red shovel in his hand and was clumsily digging up shells and sand, and tossing the mixture towards the water. His mother stood behind him, taking in the picture of her son playing on the sand, the great expanse of water stretching beyond them to the horizon. Then the mother knelt down on the warm sand and took a short video of her son as he played. When she stood up she reviewed the images of her son. The smile on her face spoke of an unconditional love for her child. The mother was appreciating the moment. How wonderful, I thought, to experience those moments when we are completely mindful of what we have. We acknowledge the purity of someone or something. And in those times we understand and appreciate our lives. In our day to day, we often forget what we have. We are in tune with our deficiencies. I seem to have more clarity these days. Things are changing, again.

. . . .

It has been two years, eleven months and fifty days since I last saw Daniel. On this cloudless afternoon I sit on Bonita Beach taking in the steady lapping of the sea hitting the shore, the high-pitch sounds of little children playing in the sand. Parents sit nearby, coaxing and encouraging.

I was back on Bonita Beach almost three years to the day when our family went out on the Gulf of Mexico for a day of boating, and a late-day picnic right here on this beach. It was also the occasion when I took the last outdoor photograph of my kids together. Since that day so much has changed.

Sitting on the beach, thinking about our life now,

without Daniel, it would have been easy to get stuck in lamenting our loss and wishing we were all together. However, in that moment I chose to recall one of our great family adventures.

On the morning of December 27, 2008, we packed up our vehicles and left the cottage early in the morning, heading home to Oakville. We were scheduled to fly out later that evening to Ft. Lauderdale, Florida, then rent a vehicle and drive two and a half hours to Bonita Springs. The plan worked well on paper, but by the time we arrived in Ft. Lauderdale, we were all exhausted. After loading our luggage, the girls and I got into the back of the truck. Bruce would do the driving and Daniel would navigate the isolated stretch of highway known as Alligator Alley. After a few minutes of conversation, I fell asleep listening to a rock music station.

When I woke up we were exiting Interstate 75 at Estero, Florida, a few minutes away from our destination. It was almost three a.m., and Daniel and Bruce were deep in conversation.

Over the years, our family had come to depend on Daniel.

Naples Beach, Florida, March 14, 2012
Today is Emily's birthday. She will be eighteen, and Daniel would have been twenty-six. We drive into Naples, Florida, to celebrate. But before dinner we decide to go to the beach in Naples to see the sunset. As we walk out onto the beach from the parking lot, I notice that we are near the spot where our family watched the sunset four years ago. Just like that night in 2008, the sun leaves a ribbon of bright purple cloud in its wake,

and so I start taking photos of Emily and her friend. Their skin is a light bronze—sun-kissed. The beach grasses bend gently in the early evening breeze. Satisfied that we have again witnessed a stunning sunset, we turn our backs on the Gulf of Mexico and walk back toward the parking lot.

Before leaving the seashore, I stop and take a long look down the beach, trying to see the image of Daniel when we were last here. The others are already ahead of me when Bruce notices me staring where our family had been. He nods, as if he, too, is seeing Daniel with us, but no words are spoken. We are here and then we are gone.

Bonita Beach, Florida, April 6, 2012
As I drive away from the beach for the last time that spring, Pearl Jam's *Black* is on the radio. "*And now my bitter hands cradle broken glass of what was everything.*" *Give sorrow words.*

I quickly reach for the dial and crank up the volume so I can be absorbed in Daniel's music.

Time heals. Grief remembers.

The End

Afterword

Postmortem

Everybody who knew Daniel was as shocked by his suicide as we were. None of us knew the other Daniel; particularly in the last months of his life. Changes in his brain functioning, chronic health conditions, and alcohol contributed to our son's bouts of mania and depression. In his last hours Daniel would not have recognized himself.

Two days after what would have been Daniel's twenty-sixth birthday, I came across a vital piece of information that had eluded me. In *The Globe* and *Mail* newspaper, I stumbled onto an article entitled: "The fragility of the teenaged brain." *The Globe* described a study, led by researchers at the University of Montreal, that claimed a blow or bruising to the frontal lobes could cause severe damage, even trauma, if it affected the cognitive part of the brain responsible for decision-making and organization responses. This vital part of the brain (known as the subcortal region) controls moods and behaviour.

Since my son's death, I had read the literature on mental illnesses, depression, and disorders of the brain. I had also reached out to clinical professionals whose day-to-day work involves diagnosing and treating diseases of the brain, including Dr. Roger McIntyre, Professor of Psychiatry and Pharmacology at the University of Toronto and Head of the Mood Disorders Psychopharmacology Unit, University Health Network in Toronto. Dr. McIntyre's research into inflammation and its connection to mood disorders is in part responsible for reshaping the model of treatment for sufferers of depression. Dr. McIntyre:

It is not uncommon because of the effect of depression on the brain that it can take the sufferer's ability to have insight and hovering capacity as to what they are going through. In other words it is the case that depression hijacks people and locks them into a reality misperception and distortion that is immutable in many cases. It is not volitional what they are doing. Most suicide is impulsive and many who survive an attempt really didn't want to do it to completion.

I had become a lay expert on depression, but I still felt as if I was missing an essential piece of information that would connect events to the changes in Daniel's behaviour. But after reading the *Globe* article, the research and studies made more sense. Daniel was an avid boarder: snowboard, longboard, and wakeboard. As an adolescent, I know he fell hard, hitting his head at high speed, particularly when he wakeboarded, possibly jarring his brain or worse, sustaining brain damage (or concussions). In the developing brain, a severe blow to the head can lead to deficits in the brain's working memory. The blow can affect a person's ability to "hold and manipulate information for short periods of time." It can also lead to impaired concentration and be the cause of severe headaches, both of which Daniel suffered.

Daniel routinely snowboarded into halfpipes to get some backside air or perform an alley-oop; rotating 180 degrees towards the up-side of the halfpipe. He lived for the high of floating above the ground. But there were times when he fell hard or slammed into the wall of the halfpipe. He adopted the same risk-taking behaviour while riding his wakeboard. Daniel would instruct me to drive the boat at twenty-two MPH while he waited for the precise moment when there was enough tension on the towrope to give him the best pop (or air) to complete his trick. Then he would attempt a big spin and land hard on the water, and sometimes his head would take the force of the fall. As the driver of the boat, I saw some of those falls; as I turned the boat around to pick him up he would wave his arm in the air, signaling he was fine, let's do it again.

We encouraged athletic participation in our family, when what we needed to be was more aware of the risks, the symptoms, and long-term side effects associated with the extreme sports that Daniel participated in.

I had also read about epigenetics, which refers to a "heritable but mutable set of processes that regulate the expression of particular genes in certain cell types and/ or at specific developmental time points." Recent studies by Poulter et al. reported "alterations in epigenetic markers in suicide victims suggesting a link between mechanisms that regulate gene expression and Major Depressive Disorder (MDD)."

Further research has shown that epigenetic modifications "can occur in response to drug abuse, stress, learning, and early life experience."

I knew that my son's asthma and anaphylaxis created a burden of anxiety that affected him all his life. One study in particular: *Chronic Physical Conditions and Their Association with First Onset of Suicidal Behavior in the World Mental Health Surveys,* confirmed what I had felt in regards to Daniel's ongoing health challenges:

Most physical conditions were associated with suicidal ideation; chronic headache, other chronic pain, and respiratory conditions were associated with attempts in the total sample. Physical conditions were especially predictive of suicidality if they occurred early in life. As the number of physical conditions increased, the risk of suicidal outcomes also increased.

And then the conclusion: "The presence of physical conditions is a risk factor for suicidal behavior *even in the absence of mental disorder.*" Kate M. Scott et al.

Much of the current research strongly links asthma and depression in a variety of findings: asthma and depression may have an "additive" adverse effect on the normal asthma-related quality-of-life reductions. Specific asthma symptoms appear to be linked to depression; sadness and depression can produce respiratory effects consistent with asthma exacerbations; depression appears to be negatively related to asthma treatment compliance; corticosteroid use in asthma treatment has been associated with depression, *Opolski & Wilson, 2005.*

In the 2000 *Behavioral Risk Factor Surveillance System Study*, asthma sufferers reported significantly more "unhealthy days both physically and mentally" than the non-sufferers—further proof that individuals who experience chronic asthmatic symptoms tend to have a reduced health-related quality of life.

. . . .

Daniel did not wake up one morning and figure he'd had enough. Life over. No, there were critical factors and important events that all played into his last day. Awful, isn't it? To realize you didn't really know what you were doing while you were raising your kids?

At least now I can point to the beginning of our son's malaise with some understanding. Daniel's fearless nature drove him to get involved in BMX biking and then into extreme boarding sports as a teenager. I know that he suffered repeated blows to his head, and if he had ever had a concussion it would have gone undiagnosed. In high school he began having sinus and migraine headaches. During this time there would have been imperceptible decreases in his brain activity, eventually leading to his inability to concentrate and to follow instruction.

We don't have absolute proof that brain injury was a factor in Daniel's death; however, what we do have is a growing body of evidence in regards to suicide, specifically in young males, that can be attributed to an undiagnosed brain injury. And if that was the case, I understand why Daniel was unable to concentrate in his first year of university. He began falling behind and feeling guilty for not going to school and then he concealed his troubles. He began drinking to alleviate his growing malaise. My son's narrative had changed between high school and his first year at university and not for the good.

Postmortem studies on suicide indicate a localized reduction in serotonin transporter binding, in the ventromedial prefrontal cortex. Specifically, this region of the brain is associated with willed action, mood, and decision making. Abnormalities increase the risk of impulsive disinhibited behaviour, which makes a high risk of suicide more likely. Research on suicidal behaviour implicates altered serotonin functions, genetics, and epigenetic and childhood adversity. (*J. J. Mann, MD and D. M. Currier, PhD.*)

What I have come to acknowledge is that Bruce and I were both responsible for our son's well-being. So it would follow that we had responsibility in his untimely death, but we couldn't help what we were unable to comprehend. Daniel had adapted all his life to health challenges. His melancholy was another problem that he would work through on his own.

So much of the literature on depression talks about a point in a person's life when "the switch" that controls depression is flipped on. The circuitry of the brain changes as a result of experiences, genetics, lifestyle, and goddamned bad luck. The switch that had been flipped set in motion the way he interpreted his experiences. Add to that his childhood chronic health conditions virtually setting him up to view himself through a negative lens. Daniel's physical health conditions were a risk factor for suicidal behaviour. Looking back, we knew nothing of synapses and brain circuitry and the catastrophic fallout from long-term depression.

Daniel was a daydreamer. Sensitive and inquisitive by nature, he was forever trying to interpret the world around him. As a young man he identified with those who were marginalized; people who were considered the underdogs. He was attracted to lyrics and literature that evoked powerful emotions: love and loss, suffering, and hope. Conceivably, Daniel was drawn to painful narratives as a way to figure out what was taking over his own life.

A final note from Dr. McIntyre

Mood disorders are prevalent, often recurrent and severe mental disorders that have their age of onset for most individuals between the ages of fifteen to thirty. The onset of depression at this time of life has a significant impact on educational attainment, occupational trajectory, personality development, interpersonal relations, and romantic life. In addition, individuals with depression find themselves at increased risk for many medical disorders that are more typically encountered in individuals of older age, i.e. cardiovascular disease, hypertension, diabetes mellitus type II. It is now known that mood disorders are the leading cause of disability in North America. It is also well established that mood disorders insufficiently treated are associated with high rates of premature mortality.

The exact causes of mood disorder are not precisely known. It is, however, agreed that a complex interaction between genetic predisposition as well as environmental stress leads to depression syndromes. It is also well documented that mood disorders are associated with changes in the structure, function, and chemical composition of the brain (and body). Along with the familiar "chemical imbalance in the brain" hypothesis, research additionally indicates that abnormalities in the body's inflammatory system and metabolic system may be causative.

The features of depression affect a person's thinking, emotions, and behaviour, as evidenced by their difficulty in interpersonal relations and the workplace. It is well established that suicidality is part of depression and in many cases, but not all, can be prevented. The most important step towards reducing tragic outcomes in depression is to reduce stigma and other barriers to healthcare and improve outcomes with available treatments. In the future, it is our hope that in addition to curing depression, we will be able to prevent the onset in the first place: These are goals that are very much within our grasp.

Grief work

Oakville, May 2, 2009

On the first Saturday after our son's suicide, the four of us got into our truck and drove into downtown Oakville to see a grief counsellor. Emily wanted nothing to do with a stranger who did not know her brother, but we convinced her to join us for this first visit. The four of us stopped when we reached her office door, wondering if we should flee. If we made a run for it maybe we could escape the avalanche of grief headed in our direction.

But we knew we needed help. So we opened the door and walked into a small waiting room decorated in soft pastel colours. Each of us sat down and waited for the grief counsellor to finish up with a client. Someone else was also dealing with grief. A kind-looking woman with short, red hair came out into the waiting room. She nodded to our family and walked a solemn middle-aged woman to the door.

"Take care. See you next week," the counsellor offered. She shut the waiting room door and introduced herself.

"Hello, I'm Sharon. Please make yourself comfortable."

I moved immediately to the chaise longue in the corner of the room. Bruce, Aimee, and Emily sat in the wing chairs placed in a semi-circle in her office suite. Then she sat down, clasped her hands together, and began to explain the grief process.

"Your overwhelming sense of loss will eventually subside," Sharon said and paused. I was surprised to see her eyes tear up. I kept my eyes on her face, hoping that she would say something to end my agony. I had never felt so lonely before.

"Sharon, I can't go on. I'm not supposed to outlive my child!"

"Lynn, this will take a tremendous effort on your part, but I can tell you that your grief work will determine how you are able to relate to the world again. Your sadness will diminish over time, but the pain will always be part of you."

"You were Daniel's mother," Sharon said.

"I will always be his mother," I said.

"You're absolutely right, Lynn. You will always be Daniel's mom."

Then Bruce spoke. "We are holding on to one another right now; before we do anything regarding Daniel we discuss it first as a family. We are trying …"

Bruce paused, his tone low and quiet. "It's so hard."

"Bruce, my heart goes out to your family," Sharon said. "I can't imagine what you're going through, but I hope that I can support all of you."

She continued. "Some people I know have found comfort in bringing their deceased children into their new lives."

Sharon had referred to Daniel as deceased. How could that be? I was still in disbelief.

"I don't understand what you're saying," I said.

"Essentially, what I'm talking about is Daniel's legacy. For example, find a quiet place in your home to display photographs of your son, a private place where you can reflect on his life and your lives as a family. I like to think of it as a retreat where you can be alone with your thoughts."

"All I can think about is sleeping," I said. "Because when I sleep I can forget that my son is never going to be coming home."

Then she took out a large piece of white paper and began drawing vertical lines, with spaces in-between the lines. The first lines indicated where we were that day. The lines were drawn very close together, which meant that we were completely absorbed in grief. Then she drew more lines; this time they were farther apart, indicating that the periods of intense grief would get shorter with time.

But that day, and for many months to come, each of us was in such deep distress that we were unable to help one another as we mourned. We tried to comfort each other, but the agonizing ache of grief is debilitating both physically and emotionally. Getting out of bed is a monumental task. It makes being present for someone else who is grieving almost impossible. I've come to think that grief is a primal and solitary experience; we need to be private to protect what is left of ourselves.

The thing with grief is that you have no control over it. A sense of desperation slips over you as if from nowhere. And the erratic nature of the emotions involved in grieving for your child make it difficult to sustain family life.

"The grief literature tells us to take all the time we

need before resuming activities." But it is also written with a big caveat: *You should not feel stuck in one place.* How long can we be absorbed by our loss? Is it a year, maybe two at tops? I don't want to stay stuck in this orbit of longing for Daniel. But for many more months, even years, I have to trust my feelings. I knew early on that I would have to immerse myself in missing Daniel in order to move towards acceptance. And I continue to do the "*grief work*", because it is the only way for me to survive the loss of our son. This is not a race for me.

Our family has now passed the fourth anniversary of Daniel's suicide. Four lonely years filled with looking back instead of forward. Staring at mothers and fathers with their sons, yearning for our old relationship with Daniel. Grieving for my son has trumped everything.

. . . .

Daniel has left us with gifts. I try each day to listen, and be clear-eyed, in order to understand what he gave us. I have learned to let go of the notion that I can control things in life. I cannot. Our son would want us to continue, and carry on our family adventures, and in that way we are honouring his life.

Letter to Daniel (part two)

.... Dear Daniel

I shook when your dad told me, "The news is not good."
Why didn't you answer our calls that night? We couldn't
figure out why you hadn't come home for dinner. When
did you last think about your family that terrible night?
Did you consider, even for a moment, that our lives would
be a living hell after you were gone? Why didn't you tell us
that you hated who you had become? You had lost hope.
Despite all of the good in your life, I think there was a lay-
er of fear and uncertainty that left you adrift, especially
when you went away to university.

You had turned twenty-three in March of 2009, and I
was beginning to feel less worried about you. You seemed
to be managing your asthma and allergies, so I could step
back and not focus on your day-to-day health. But I know
that you had become so expert at hiding your frustrations
with your allergies that we rarely discussed them that
year.

I believe now that you did try to reach out to me. Only
now can I hear the echoes of your screams. Whenever I
walk into the cottage, I can feel your despair. If we had
any idea about your struggles at university or college, we

would have supported you. But of course you didn't want to disappoint us. You despised the fact that you were lying to us, and so you unleashed the anger on yourself, which ended with your suicide. What a fucking waste of life, Daniel! Your family and your friends would have intervened, but we didn't have the chance to know the other young man who you had become. And there must have been time, before a raging suicidal ideation took control of you, when you would have thought that you could manage your emotional pain. The two Daniels in a battle to live or die.

In the last years of your life you struggled with relationships with friends and family, in part because you sealed off your emotional self. On the outside you appeared as if you didn't care about others. I saw through that, but I didn't know that your behaviour was symptomatic of someone not coping with life. That Daniel was a stranger to us. You were full of shame about what you perceived as failures. That led you on a treacherous path towards self-destruction.

By the spring of 2009, no one around you could penetrate your protective shield, and without professional support, you were unable to shed your troubled thoughts. You did not have to die. This is our tragedy.

You acted out of desperation and the pain of your double life. On your final day, as you became tangled in a web of hopelessness, you may have felt that we would be better off without you. You had exhausted all of the energy it took to appear as if nothing was wrong, when you were actually crumbling.

It is painful to think of you at our cottage alone, ruminating on what had gone wrong in your life. You had *transformed into the other Daniel, thinking and then acting upon the tortured notions he had of himself.*

You were the archetypal male—handsome and athletic. Strong on the outside, gentle and caring at your core. You were sensitive to our emotions, and often brought calm when fear and doubt crept into our lives.

Your suicide will haunt us the rest of our lives. Your life was wiped out in minutes, and now memories have taken your place. I was despondent for a very long time, but I could not carry on in isolation every day. So I went in search of answers. I wanted to understand the pain and the despair you must have felt. I had to make sense of our loss. I had to accept that you would not be coming home.

I love you, forever and always, Mom xo

Acknowledgements

I could not have written this book without the love and support of my family. My husband, Bruce, who encouraged my writing because he knew it was where I found peace. Aimee, my oldest daughter, a graduate of literature, was the first reader of this work. You have wisdom beyond your years. And Emily, thank you for your willingness to talk about your brother. You bring joy into our lives.

I am immensely proud of my family for their courage and for allowing me to take them back to the hardest days. I hope that the love we share is what you remember most.

To my parents, I love you.

Give Sorrow Words began during the summer of 2010 on the dock at our cottage. Under blue summer skies I began the journey to understand our son's depression and suicide.

During that summer I attended the Humber School for Writers Summer Workshop, where I met my first author/mentor, Miriam Toews. Thank you for reminding me that this was important work. During the fall of that year I continued writing my manuscript under the guidance of author Susan Swan, to whom I owe a debt of gratitude for nurturing the writer within, and for introducing me to David Bennett of The Transatlantic Agency, who championed my book and whose counsel I relied on to get this book published.

A special note of thanks to the following people: editors Kathryn Cole and Patricia Ocampo. Authors Wayson Choy and Larry Hill, whose literary advice I will never forget. Dr. Roger McIntyre, for sharing his research into depression and disorders of the brain. Dr.

Sol Stern, for his encouragement and interest in this book. Sharon Lowe, M.Ed., for sharing her research on grief. Kathy Short, Ph.D., C.Psych. and Dr. Ian Manion for their generosity and constructive criticism.

Special thanks to Daniel's friends who offered their recollections. It is a window into our son's life that we cherish. Alex, for sharing an important part of her life. I know it was not easy to do.

I remain grateful to John and Pam Newton and their family and our Muskoka neighbours.

To the early readers of my work, and to those who remained present for our family, especially Colleen Semkiw, Laura Klemenchuk, Jan Stern, Janice McClelland, Julia Mori, Laurel Brooks, Suzanne Robinson, Janet Shaughnessy, Carole Latour and others. Thank you.

In the end, writing a memoir is the culmination of hundreds of conversations, meditations, and acts of kindness. To everyone who knew Daniel and supported our family and this book, you have my deepest gratitude.

Daniel's inner thoughts, highlighted in italics throughout the book, were a result of my conversations with him and others. The benefit of time, education and reflection has allowed me to better understand the stigma and emotional pain associated with depression.

Finally,
To my son, Daniel

You taught me how to be your mom, and in loving you I learned to see the wonder and beauty in all children. You showed me how to enjoy the moments and experiences that bring joy.

You have been with me every day, as I wrote in the silence of a snowstorm or in the places that we once visited as a family. Regardless of where I wrote, I felt your presence. In writing your story I was able to go back to our old life, when we were a family of five.

Further Reading

Baird, Jean. Bowering, George. *The Heart Does Break: Canadian Writers on Grief and Mourning.* Toronto: Random House Canada. 2009. Print.

Jamison, Kay Redfield. *Night Falls Fast: Understanding Suicide.* New York: Random House, Inc. 1999. Print.

Joiner, Thomas. *Why People Die by Suicide.* Cambridge: President and Fellows (Harvard Corporation). 2005. Print.

Levine, Stephen. *Unattended Sorrow: Recovering From Loss and Reviving the Heart.* Emmaus: Rodale Inc. 2005. Print.

Shakur, Tupac. *The Rose that Grew from Concrete.* New York: Pocket Books, a division of Simon & Schuster Inc. 1999. Print.

Styron, William. *Darkness Visible: A Memoir of Madness.* New York: Random House, Inc.1990. Print.

Toews, Miriam. *Swing Low: A Life.* Toronto: Random House of Canada. 2005. Print.

Shakespeare, William. *The Tragedy of Macbeth.* (Act IV, scene 3, line 4.). England: Publisher, Henry Condell, and John Heminges. First Folio edition, 1623.

Credits

Audioslave. "I Am the Highway". Epic, 2004.

Baz Luhrmann. "Everybody's Free (To Wear Sun-screen)". *Something for Everybody*. EMI, 1999.

Bob Marley. "Redemption Song". *Uprising*. Island/Tuff

Gong, 1980. Pearl Jam. "The End". *Backspacer*. Monkeywrench, 2009.

Pearl Jam. "Black". *Ten*. Epic, 1991.

Pink Floyd. "Comfortably Numb". *The Wall*. Harvest (UK)- Columbia (US), 1980.

The Tragically Hip. "Bobcaygeon". *Phantom Power*. Universal, 1998.

Praise for *Give Sorrow Words*

Lynn Keane's searing quest to understand the suicide of her 23-year-old son led her through the labyrinth of her own grief and then, to the latest research on brain injury and adolescent depression. Her conclusions shed welcome light on this darkest of all family tragedies.

Susan Mahoney, Executive producer,
The Sunday Edition, CBC Radio.

In Give Sorrow Words, Lynn Keane eloquently and poignantly details her journey to find answers, consolation and a legacy after her son unexpectedly takes his life. While her story especially resonates with those of us who have lost a child, it will also increase awareness of a pervasive problem in our world, and provide strength, support and new ideas for those who have a child struggling with mental illness.

Frank van Nie
Past Board Chair,
Canadian Mental Health Association/Peel Branch

Lynn Keane is an author and former broadcast journalist. Since the sudden passing of her son Daniel in 2009, Keane has dedicated her life to sharing her family's story, educating about the underlying causes of depression and the importance of treating mental illness.

Her work has been featured in *The National Post, The Globe & Mail,* and *Moods Magazine, CBC* and *TVO*'s The Agenda with Steve Paikin.

Through advocacy, an open approach, and working with mental health professionals and organizations, Keane has become a passionate, highly respected voice on depression and suicide prevention in Canada. She lives with her family in Oakville, Ontario.

For further information, visit lynnkeane.ca

Author photo Alex Albojer

CPSIA information can be obtained at www.ICGtesting.com
Printed in the USA
LVOW08s1951250714

396042LV00001B/33/P